The
BEATING SHYNESS
Workbook

Dena Michelli

Dedication

This is for the people who told their stories of being shy for this workbook – and for others who have similar stories.

This book is also for my family. My heartfelt gratitude and love goes to you.

I am including my family of friends, at home and abroad, to this dedication. You have housed me, holidayed me, supported me and accepted me unequivocally. You know who you are and I am privileged and thankful to count you among my inner circle.

Shyness is a miserable condition. It commands too much space and masks the potential of those who are afflicted by it. The material in this workbook aims to bring hope and self-mastery to those who have the courage to step away from their habitual patterns of behaviour and try something new. It is designed to reverse the enslavement to random events and bring choice and control back to where it belongs. So this book is for you, the reader, with the greatest compassion and wish that you'll find a better way.

Dena Michelli is a leadership development specialist who was awarded a Ph.D for her work on transformational personal development. She works as an executive coach and designs and facilitates leadership programmes, mostly through university business schools with international audiences. In her spare time, she writes and makes stained glass windows.

The
BEATING SHYNESS
Workbook

Dena Michelli

First published in Great Britain in 2014 by Hodder & Stoughton. An Hachette UK company.

First published in US in 2014 by The McGraw-Hill Companies, Inc.

This edition published 2014

Copyright © Dena Michelli 2014

British Library Cataloguing in Publication Data: a catalogue record for this title is available from the British Library.

Library of Congress Catalog Card Number: on file.

10 9 8 7 6 5 4 3 2 1

Cover credit © Alan Bailey / Getty Images

Typeset by Cenveo® Publisher Services.

Printed and bound in Great Britain by CPI Group (UK) Ltd., Croydon, CRO 4YY.

Paperback ISBN 978 1 473 600300 0

Hodder & Stoughton policy is to use papers that are natural, renewable and recyclable products and made from wood grown in sustainable forests. The logging and manufacturing processes are expected to conform to the environmental regulations of the country of origin.

Hodder & Stoughton Ltd

338 Euston Road

London NW1 3BH

www.hodder.co.uk

Acknowledgements

There are some people who have been pivotal in inspiring the material in this workbook and sharing their stories, thoughts and ideas about overcoming shyness.

So, for the stories, I'd like to convey my thanks to Rose, Isaac, Elizabeth, Anne, Herbert, Kate, Vanessa, Andrew, Maisie and Robert. (These are not their real names. I use them for the purposes of confidentiality.)

My thanks also to Paul Hiltermann who introduced me (virtually) to Henk T van der Molen. Together, they undertook research and created a programme to help shy people take control of their lives. Their frame inspires one of the central pillars of this workbook, for which I am thankful.

Contents

Introduction to this workbook

If you have picked up this book, it is likely that you have a personal interest in overcoming shyness. This may be for you, or it may be for someone else close to you for whom shyness is a problem. Whether you enter this workbook for yourself, or on behalf of someone in your close circle, it is designed to build greater understanding of shyness as a phenomenon and point towards ways of dealing with it that will diminish its effect.

In exploring the territory of shyness, and in speaking to many people who experience being shy, it seems that this condition is quite common. Many people feel shy at times. Some people feel shy in specific circumstances, perhaps when they are making a presentation or asking someone to dance at a club. Others feel shy most of the time. Wherever you fall on this continuum, there will be something in this workbook for you.

Most of us learn from experience and it is our formative childhood experiences (and the way we make sense of them) that lay down the foundations for our social behaviour. We learn how not to behave, because it elicits 'punishment' and we learn how to behave because it elicits 'reward'. Our expectation of 'reward' or 'punishment' influences our behaviour in our adult years and creates the social patterns that we are known by. (The term 'punishment' is not literal – necessarily. It merely means that something that you want is not available to you or is taken from you. This may be your dignity, your pocket money, a treat, inclusion in a group and so on. The term 'reward' is not literal either – necessarily. It may be a feeling of being praised or validated, a privilege, a sense of belonging and so on. These 'rewards' may also be referred to as 'positive strokes'.)

When we feel that we are controlled by our behaviours, such as our shyness, we may just 'give up' and learn to live with the feelings and disappointments that occur as a result. However, if we get into a position where we can control our behaviours, or master our emotional landscape, a whole new future opens up before us and we can move into our lives with an increased degree of optimism, confidence and freedom.

It is the purpose of this workbook, therefore, to enable you to clear your path of your old behavioural detritus; detritus that was strewn before you could think about its consequences, and put you in the driving seat of your own life. This is not to suggest that you'll learn to 'act' as if you were in the driving seat, but that you'll be genuinely equipped to 'be' in the driving seat. For this to happen, you need to tap into your own personality and manage your social choices in a conscious way; a way that will allow your 'authentic' self to emerge rather than a hidden or filtered version of yourself.

So, this workbook is written with a diverse audience in mind.

There is something for those who like to reflect upon and analyse situations to derive a greater theoretical understanding of them. These people will be likely to conceive new approaches in the context of their analysis, thinking through the various outcomes that may stem from a different set of responses that they may now choose.

There is something for those who like to experiment with new behaviours in order to test them out and see what happens.

There is something for those who like to roll their sleeves up and just do things differently. These people like to test themselves in real time, so to speak, not wasting their efforts on reflecting and experimenting.

Finally, there is something for those who like to observe and reflect upon others' styles and approaches. These people like to collect examples of what works for others and decide whether they could adopt them, credibly, for themselves.

You may recognize your preferred leaning style in one of these descriptions above or you may feel that you do a little bit of all of them. Whichever preference(s) you hold, there is something in this workbook for you. So, pick and choose and go with your intuition when you are working through the different chapters.

You don't need to go through each chapter sequentially. You can dip in and dip out according to your needs. As it is a workbook, each chapter will stand in its own right and deliver the material specific to the topic under discussion. However, make this a working document. Highlight those things that strike you as relevant. Fill in the questionnaires, reflect on the prompts and use the tables and lists to keep track of your views and feelings. Also, don't be reticent to write in the margins, annotate the text or disagree with what is being said. Personalize this workbook so that you can capture and retain your learning.

If, however, you prefer a different format, think about how you'd like to capture and record your experiences and keep your nose to the grindstone. Perhaps a journal or video diary would be more suitable for you. Alternatively, you may prefer to create a spreadsheet for yourself – or make a project plan. You may also consider working through the exercises with a trusted friend who is tackling shyness themselves. Or get yourself a coach; someone who is 'on your side' and prepared to listen to you as you reflect on and digest the results of your practice. Whatever your preference, at the end of each chapter you are given a framework to capture your learning. You might like to make this a discipline so that you are ready to move on to the next challenge having distilled everything you can from the one you've just grappled with. We all have different ways of making sense of our learning journeys so pick one that works for you.

Whether with a friend or on your own, it is advised that you do the exercises that are recommended and that you practise the behavioural alternatives that you select for yourself. The old adage 'practice makes perfect' really does carry an important message. This expression has been updated by Malcolm Gladwell in his book *Outliers: The Story of Success*. In this work, Gladwell advocates spending 10,000 hours in practice to become an expert. (He calls this the '10,000 hour rule'.) So, imagine how confident you could be if you spent 10,000 hours practising your social skills and developing your social facility.

There are stories from other people in this workbook. These will be used to help you consider what you would have done if you'd been in their shoes – and to reassure you that you are not alone. When we observe others performing well, we generally assume that 'It's OK for them. They don't have to overcome being shy!' However, this is a fantasy, and this fantasy may be creating a sizeable obstacle for you to overcome. If you think you're the only one who's suffering from shyness, you put yourself under incredible pressure to deliver a more confident social demeanour in order to 'catch' or 'match' others' positions. However, believe it or not, most people are not as confident as they appear. They have their own demons to conquer and are probably struggling just as much as you are. If you focus less on the assumed difference between you and everyone else, you may find that the obstacles to your success diminish significantly.

Here is a synopsis of the chapters so that you can plan your route through this workbook.

→ Part I – Getting your head around the theory and dynamics of shyness

Chapter 1 – Why am I shy? This will be an exploration of the territory on which shyness sits. (Shyness may also be referred to as social phobia or social anxiety disorder.) This chapter builds your understanding of shyness so that you can approach your condition more openly. You are encouraged to think about the perceptions you hold that may prevent you from making any changes and you are introduced to what the geneticists and psychologists are saying on the topic. To help you approach your exploration more precisely, you are also introduced to the four generally accepted categories of shyness: Circumstantial, Behavioural, Emotional and Rational.

Chapter 2 – How shy are you? Where are you on the Shyness-Boldness continuum? Once you have developed an understanding of your particular version of shyness, you are encouraged to think about what you need to do differently to ensure that your shyness is not debilitating, what you're motivated to change and how you are going to do so. In this way, you can then define your own success criteria and use the action planning template to help you identify a meaningful goal.

Chapter 3 – What kind of shy are you? This chapter enables you to explore the nature of your own form of shyness. This is done through the completion of a questionnaire. The four different forms of shyness are used to clarify where you need to place your attention for the best results because each of these four bases of shyness has different manifestations in different circumstances. By getting your head around the precise kind of shyness you suffer from, you will be able to seek and celebrate those moments that do not call you into your shyness. You will also be able to develop and build new approaches that enable you to attain higher levels of social confidence.

Chapter 4 – What are the primary and secondary gains from being shy? Although you may not wish to swallow the notion that shyness brings benefits, this will be explained and explored so that you can examine your motivation to maintain your shyness. By looking at the 'paybacks' – the primary and secondary gains – you will be able to decide whether or not you want to perpetuate your shyness. (The terms 'primary' and 'secondary' gains are explained fully in Chapter 4.)

Chapter 5 – When am I not shy? We all have stories to tell of ourselves in 'flow'; those moments when we have overcome our natural inhibitions and triumphed in our endeavours. There are seeds of inspiration in these stories; seeds that can be harvested and grown. By developing a battery of 'good' stories that inspire different responses in you, you can choose your reactions and develop new skills that will provide a safety net for every eventuality – and build long-term confidence.

Chapter 6 – What triggers my shyness? Most of us have a series of sabotaging messages, scripts or crumple buttons that go round and round in our head. These can get so loud that we can't even imagine being free to make our own behavioural choices. Generally, these come from our childhood and are triggered by circumstances that are similar to those we encountered as a child. For instance, if you were instructed to 'be charming to our guests' as you handed round the creamed mushroom vol-au-vents and were told that you were 'useless' if you didn't do this to the satisfaction of your parents, every time you entertain guests, you may hear this disempowering message.

→ Part II – Getting practical about developing the skills to overcome shyness

In Part II, you are invited to think about what strategies you might invent to help you deal with the four different types of shyness. The first of these will be dealing with situationally specific forms of shyness.

Chapter 7 – How to deal with circumstantial shyness Circumstantial or situational shyness occurs on specific occasions and can 'buck the trend' of your usual confident personality. When there are high levels of ambiguity, complexity and freedom, the choices you make are clearly visible and likely to attract attention and comment. It is on these occasions, in the absence of tried and tested 'rules of engagement', that shyness often strikes. This chapter contains stories and ideas on:

▶ Making presentations or giving a performance
▶ Dealing with interviews or socially charged situations (where you are at risk of rejection)

Chapter 8 – How to deal with behavioural shyness To continue the practical theme, Chapter 8 focuses on the behavioural type of shyness. This form of shyness is defined by a kind of social ineptitude that results in severe inhibition. This may include: a reluctance to initiate a conversation, an inability to ask for what you need and avoidance of making choices that go against someone else's will. Indeed, someone suffering in this way may engage in many other 'avoidance behaviours' to protect them from having to enter the cut and thrust of social engagement.

To help you in your behavioural shyness, you are encouraged to adopt a helpful questioning approach, build a range of adaptive behaviours and command your body language so that you feel 'in control' of the interaction. Specifically, this chapter includes:

▶ Managing your body
▶ Placing your attention beyond yourself so that you can take your focus off your shyness
▶ Listening with curiosity and asking great questions
▶ Understanding spatial etiquette

Chapter 9 – How to deal with emotional shyness This chapter will focus on the emotional form of shyness that manifests in the physiology of one's body. Typically, this shows up as the 'fight' or 'flight' response. Whatever the trigger that is perceived to require an urgent response, the body is put into a state of alert and infused with the chemicals that support 'staying in' (aggressively) or 'getting out' (rapidly).

Specifically this chapter helps you to:

▶ Understand more about what happens in situations charged with emotional shyness
▶ Identify strategies that enable you to put yourself into settings that usually trigger a shy response
▶ Manage your physiological response to emotional shyness

Chapter 10 – How to deal with 'rational' shyness Having tackled shyness in the circumstantial, behavioural and emotional domains, this chapter moves into the thinking domain. Although the term 'rational' has been used to describe this form of shyness, it is only 'rational' inasmuch as it occurs in the thinking space and is rooted in (what is considered by the shy person) a logical and reasoned analysis. However, this thinking may be beset with leaps of abstraction and faulty reasoning that punch holes in its logical integrity. By rooting out the source of these distortions, and by disciplining the mind to obey a different thinking protocol, this form of shyness may be overcome.

In this chapter, you learn about:

▶ The vicious cycle that keeps you in the thrall of your shyness
▶ The Ladder of Inference – a thinking process that allows you to challenge and re-wire your mental circuitry
▶ The importance of staying present – not rooted in the past or speculating about the future

Chapter 11 – Adopting and maintaining new habits to overcome shyness Having completed an exploration of the different forms of shyness, you should be in a position to know yourself better, to understand the habitual patterns that undermine you and to find some solutions that can enable you to build social confidence. But how do you form and maintain your new habits? In this chapter, we start pulling together the strands to help you embed your strategies for overcoming shyness. Specifically, this chapter covers:

▶ Understanding the nature of habits

▶ Using your self-knowledge to outwit your sabotaging tendencies

▶ Establishing long-lasting and life-changing social behaviours

Chapter 12 – Bringing it all together This final chapter collects together some of the most helpful tools and techniques for each of the four domains of shyness to help you take forward the messages that have been developed throughout the workbook.

By demystifying 'shyness' and learning to be proactive and disciplined, not only will you have addressed your shyness but also you will have the added bonus of feeling much more confident and able to manage the unexpected situations that you may face in your life.

Activity 1

Where am I starting from?

This workbook leads you through a personal and practical exploration to help you create a tailored solution to overcoming your shyness. Before you set off, however, have a think about where you're starting from in terms of how you think about yourself and how others perceive you. If you don't know what they think, ask them for feedback. Pick someone you trust and ask them something like:

▶ **How would you describe my social style?**

▶ **What impact do I have?**

▶ **What conclusions do you draw from observing me in a social setting?**

It might help to write down your reflections so that your starting point is clear (a template is suggested below). This will also help you mark your progress and measure your success as you develop new skills and build more social confidence.

	This is who I am (These are the attributes you know you harbour somewhere inside but they don't often get a chance to show themselves.)	**This is what people see** (These are the attributes that people see in me.)
My social style		
The impact I have		
The perceptions that people hold of me		

Where to next?

 In this chapter, you've been introduced to how this workbook will assist you in beating your shyness and you've been given a roadmap so that you can pick and choose where you enter the field. You've also been encouraged to reflect on your learning style so that you can pick out the exercises that suit you best and you've been urged to gather feedback from your trusted circle so that you know where you're starting from.

Next, you will be encouraged to think about how you perceive your form of shyness and how you might see the positive elements of it. You are also given a brief overview of psychologists' thinking about shyness, particularly in terms of the 'nature-nurture' debate. Some of the classic misconceptions about shyness will be quashed too. In order to make your exploration more precise, you are introduced to the four forms of shyness that are generally accepted to describe the field: circumstantial, behavioural, emotional and rational.

This is the beginning of taking control of yourself so that you can favour your choices and decisions with confidence. So, now you've fired the starting gun, you'll embark on a process of enquiry that will help you understand the extent of your shyness and the specific type of shyness that affects you.

Part I

Getting your head around the theory and dynamics of shyness

① Why am I shy?

Welcome to your work on shyness! Well done for making the commitment to take charge of this debilitating social style.

Having picked up this workbook, you will be supported in your efforts to change your responses to people and situations so that you can acquire the kind of confidence that will take you into any social setting.

Throughout this book, you will be given lots of exercises to do and things to think about to help you on your way. But let's begin by setting the scene. In this chapter, you find answers to the following questions:

▶ What is shyness?
▶ What makes you shy?

→ What is shyness?

Shyness is a social disposition that afflicts many people in one circumstance or another. It might be described as 'resistance to put oneself into a situation that is perceived to carry a threat', whether it be on a one-to-one basis or a one-to-group basis. The 'threat' is likely to be connected to a fear that you'll make a fool of yourself and be revealed as lacking in something – knowledge, confidence, power, savoir-faire and so on.

Often, people tell themselves a story about what will happen when they put themselves into a social frame. For instance, they might say: 'I won't know what to say if my boss asks for my opinion in front of the team and then she'll think I don't know what I'm doing and then I'll be overlooked when her succession is being considered'; or 'Why is it whenever I want to impress someone I get completely tongue-tied and prove myself to be a total fool!' This internal narrative can become so daunting that the smallest social act becomes almost impossible. In these instances, the mind is dominated by fear of the *assumed* consequences rather than engaging with what is currently taking place. In other words, an imagined and very dark future overshadows what is happening in the present.

If being shy is your pattern, it can be experienced as one of the most disabling features of your life. It can hold you back from expressing your full potential. It can prevent you from engaging socially and enjoying the cut and thrust of banter with your friends – or prospective friends. It can isolate you and make you feel as if you're on the outside looking in at everyone else who is enjoying social adequacy or it can make you feel horribly exposed, as if everyone is looking at you and judging your social ineptitudes.

For some, shyness is perceived to be a personality trait; generally that of introversion, although this is not statistically correlated.

The difference between introverts and extraverts, according to Carl J Jung, is the place that individuals go to replenish their lost energy. Introverts tend to focus on their internal world and recharge their batteries in solitary pursuits such as reading, walking or listening to music. Whereas extraverts tend to focus on the external world and recharge their batteries by being in the midst of a social throng, playing team sports or engaging in a group activity. By virtue of their withdrawal from the social mêlée, introverts are often considered shy but this may not be prompted by shyness, merely a desire to be alone and to recharge their batteries.

Additionally, introverts tend to think in order to know what to say and extroverts tend to speak in order to know what they think. An introvert's *apparent* reluctance to give voice to their thoughts is another compounding characteristic that makes them appear shy. Yet this appearance is likely to be a product of their need to access what's going on inside their head before speaking out about it.

The source of the confusion is clear therefore. Because introversion and shyness share the same impression of social withdrawal, they tend to get conflated. However, it is important not to confuse the two or we are in danger of pigeonholing all introverts as shy (and all extraverts as socially bold) – and this is not so. Indeed, it is quite possible to be a 'gregarious introvert', for instance, or a 'shy extravert'. To add another layer of complexity, it is also possible to be shy in some circumstances but fully confident in others. So, for example, giving a speech or presentation might be easy for those who are shy in social settings, just as giving a stirring performance can be the preserve of shy actors.

Technically, shyness can be referred to as a social anxiety disorder, social phobia or 'sub-assertiveness', among other epithets, some of which are listed below:

Timid, cautious, wary, nervous, afraid, fearful, reluctant, wallflower, bashful, embarrassed, humble, self-deprecating, withdrawn, retiring, inhibited, reticent, reserved, quiet, coy, modest, demure, diffident, timorous, faint-hearted, frightened, tentative, apprehensive, hesitant, nervy, over-sensitive, undecided, doubtful, uncertain, unsure, indefinite, ambiguous, insecure, unconfident, anxious, embarrassed, humiliated, thoughtful, introverted, guarded, wary, restrained, chary, cagey, suspicious, defended, shielded, fortified, safeguarded, protected, remote, inaccessible, locked-in, secluded, sheltered, hidden, frightened, unhappy, depressed, antisocial, aloof, self-distasteful, self-consciousness, self-important, uptight, anal, self-obsessed, self-regarding, self-protective, apprehensive, averse, backward, circumspect, mysterious, disingenuous, disinclined, distrustful, loner, sheepish, shrinking violet, suspicious, unassertive, unassured, unresponsive, antisocial, priggish, superior, apologetic, submissive, flustered, meek, demurring, disciplined, 'good', unimposing, accommodating, boring, undemanding, unable to say 'No!', wouldn't say boo to a goose!

.... or some other derogatory term!

(Before we feel that we are carrying all the negative characteristics or behavioural projections as shy people, perhaps we should remind ourselves that the opposite of shyness is often equally derogative: brash, over-confident, arrogant, bullying, insensitive, egotistical…)

Activity 1.1

How would *you* describe shyness?

These are the terms I associate with being shy:	

*These are the words
I would use to describe
my form of shyness:*

You may have come up with some different terms that you feel describe your particular form of shyness more accurately so do substitute them for the ones used as you read so that 'the shyness conversation' is meaningful to you and you can work with it creatively. For ease of reading, however, the words 'shy' and 'shyness' will be adopted to describe an 'awkwardness or excessive self-consciousness in front of people'. (Occasionally, there will be a replacement that conveys similar meaning.) This definition of shyness is not to override your preferred version but to prepare a benign canvas onto which you can add your own colour.

More importantly, the whole point of this book is to get you to a place where *you are able to manage your shyness rather than let your shyness manage you*. This aspiration supersedes any definition of the term. So, rather than being academic, we take a more practical view and use generally accepted terms.

And there is a kinder light we can throw on the terms that are used to describe shyness. Through a 'reframe', we can illuminate the more positive aspects of our social timidity rather than obfuscate these in our wholesale dislike of this trait. A reframe merely takes a different perspective view and allows a shift in your mindset. Let's take some examples. Someone who is considered to be reserved, for instance, may be perceived to be thoughtful (positive, +ve) or aloof (negative, −ve). Someone who is considered to be bold may be perceived as confident (+ve) or arrogant (−ve). Someone who is considered to be imaginative may be perceived to be creative (+ve) or on another planet! (−ve). And someone who is considered to be shy may be perceived to be 'modest', 'sensitive' or 'dignified'. Have a think about the terms you use to describe your own form of shyness and see whether you can illuminate the positive elements of this term by viewing it from a different perspective; by reframing it.

What words would you use to describe your form of shyness?

From Activity 1.1 – These are the words I would use to describe my form of shyness:	If I were to reframe these words positively, these are the terms I would use:

Hopefully, you will see that every characteristic or behaviour has a positive, as well as a negative, tone. In the same way that every coin has two sides, there are two sides to the qualities, capabilities and characteristics that we embody. The art is to ensure that they are known to us, integrated into our personalities and managed in a way that we choose.

Before we go any further into the whys and wherefores of your shyness, let's look at some of the thinking in this territory.

→ What the psychologists are saying

Shyness, an inclination that is found in some but not in others, has not attracted very much remedial attention in the past. It was, perhaps, regarded as a self-indulgent weakness and the way through was to muster all one's personal qualities and 'cure' oneself with pure strength of character and personal determination. This was a harsh challenge for those who were not gifted with high levels of confidence in social situations and it often led to 'avoiding behaviours' such as staying away from communal gatherings, hiding behind an acceptable role or clinging on to a confident friend.

However, theories of shyness have emerged in the more recent past and have tended to join the 'nature-nurture' debate, a debate that dominates the field in the origins of personality. In other words, are we victim to the unique set of genetic combinations that we inherit through our blood line or are the influences of our environment wholly responsible for shaping us – or does the formation of our personality fall somewhere between the two extremes. This debate has raged for years and the movement up and down the continuum of 'nature' and 'nurture' has varied according to the times.

NATURE

One of the early theories of shyness was at the deterministic end of the scale. This claimed that the shy were born with a congenital inclination to avoid situations they found menacing. Developmental psychologist Jerome Kagan Ph.D spent his career studying emotion and the stability of temperament. He suggested that about one third of shy adults had temperaments that predisposed them to this condition as infants; that is, before 'nurture' had time to have an effect. In his longitudinal studies, such infants were found to be hypersensitive to stimuli that included unknown people, objects and events. This hypersensitivity gave rise to psychological and physiological signs of fear and, as these infants grew, they showed increased brain wave activity in the right frontal lobe; the birthplace of anxiety and distress. In order to minimize their symptoms, such children tended to avoid situations that triggered the fear response, thereby appearing inhibited and shy. Added to which, parents of these children may have over-protected them, compounding these inclinations – inclinations that tended to follow them into adolescence. It has also been postulated that generalized social anxiety disorder – a general dislike of social situations – is passed down the family line, whereas non-generalized anxiety disorder, where there are specific instances of shyness, is not.

Professor Johnson at Birkbeck College, University of London, which harbours one of the world's leading baby labs, has found that babies as young as four months old recognize faces and are able to discriminate on the basis of familiarity and friendliness. Separately, it has been argued that this early sensitivity lays the foundation for the development of social skills. Professor Jennifer Urbano Blackford of Vanderbilt University, through functional magnetic resonance imaging (fMRI,) found that people who had an inhibited temperament failed to become familiar with new faces on their repeated presentation whereas people who did not have an inhibited temperament, quickly became familiar with the faces and adapted their response accordingly. She concluded that people whose responses are undifferentiated may find meeting new people overwhelming and avoid circumstances in which this is likely to happen.

Quantitative genetics embraces research into the behavioural patterns of adopted children (environmental influences of shyness) as well as identical and fraternal twins (genetic inheritance of shyness). This adds to the debate on whether or not shyness is inherited. One major study of twins done by the University of Colorado and Pennsylvania State University observed both identical and fraternal twins at 14 and 20 months. In this study, the data suggested that genetic inheritance does indeed contribute to the baby's tendency to cling to its mother when encountering a stranger. This genetic influence, the researchers suggest, accounts for at least half the foundation of shyness.

The human body carries its genetic material on 46 chromosomes, which are made up of 23 pairs. (The 23rd pair is what determines our gender. The others are undifferentiated in the male and female body.) The chromosome of particular interest to scientists who are seeking the genetic root of shyness is chromosome 11. This chromosome carries two genes, which may be present in a long or short form, that control the influence on the body of the neurotransmitters dopamine and serotonin, both of which are known to affect a person's mood.

In the case of the gene that governs the number of dopamine receptors, studies have correlated the length of the gene with shy behaviour. The long form of the gene results in lower receptivity to dopamine in certain parts of the brain (because there are fewer dopamine receptors). This relates to a lack of motivation and initiative; behaviours found in shy people. The short form of the gene equates to higher levels of receptivity of dopamine (because there are more dopamine receptors in the brain) and suggests someone who is restless and seeks novelty; a bolder person.

In the case of serotonin, Geneticist Dean Hamer of the National Institutes of Health found that low self-confidence and shyness were associated with a shorter version of the serotonin transporter promoter gene, which he called the 'anxiety gene', resulting in less serotonin activity. Higher levels of activity in the amygdala in those who are anxious and fearful has also been found to be associated with the short version of the serotonin transporter promoter gene. This additionally supports the proposition that the short version of the gene is common in those who are shy.

The genetics of shyness is still contentious, however, and repeated studies do not necessarily yield the same conclusions. However, Hamer is now presiding over an extensive piece of further research into the effects of genetics on shyness through examining and analysing the DNA of hundreds of shy children. His research team is optimistic that this will prove that the susceptibility to shyness is, at least in part, inherited.

People in the 'talking professions' (psychotherapists, counsellors, coaches) who are faced with clients seeking to rid themselves of their shy disposition have found that they can help them overcome their shyness, or at least come to terms with it, merely by informing them that their shyness is innate. Although deterministic in essence, this message seems to enable people to put their concerns to one side and just get on with getting on.

A note of caution about genetic determinism though: Professor Robert Winston, a British medical doctor and television producer, warns that this type of deterministic science negates the effects of epigenetics ('spurious' changes in the expression of a gene that is not driven by the underlying DNA). The unknown factors that can affect the function of the genome, he asserts, are much more important than is currently recognized.

It is from here that we venture into the world of 'nurture'.

NURTURE

Counter to the more deterministic theories rooted in 'nature', some have suggested that shyness is learned in our formative years – 'nurture'. It may be that shy adults had an insecure attachment to their parents as children, making them nervy and anxious. This creates a vicious cycle in which the child's relating expectations with adults is dogged by feelings of inevitable rejection. In addition to the quality of parental attachment, other childhood experiences shape their social confidence. Being bullied or teased at school tends to embed a habitual withdrawal from social situations. In this particular instance, shyness is a coping mechanism that protects the child from further abuse and enables them to survive, after a fashion. In adulthood, this coping mechanism may extend to seeking 'chemical confidence' through drinking alcohol or taking recreational drugs.

Beyond this, we may be encouraged into shyness through cultural influences. For instance, Philip G. Zimbardo, Professor Emeritus of Psychology at Standford University, studied shyness among students in different cultures and found that 60 per cent of students in Japan and Taiwan were shy whereas it was only true of 30 per cent in Israel. Digging further to the root cause of this, he found that the crucial difference was the way students' parents had attributed blame or praise. In Asia, children are encouraged to develop a modest and quiet demeanour while in Israel – and generally in the West – children are encouraged to be more articulate, assertive, individualistic and bold. These behavioural recipes work in their own cultures and, if you think about the attributes that are celebrated in Western cultures, you see that they include sociability and proactivity – the opposite of shyness – making shyness aberrant in the West. Also, the heroes (assumed to embody these qualities) are the musicians, politicians, actors and other 'winners'.

Gender differences, too, may be environmentally determined. Girls, perhaps, are more protected as infants, preventing them from developing assertive qualities, while boys are generally encouraged to be more outgoing and confident. However, boys tend to feel shyer in adolescence due, it is thought, to male role expectations.

As well as carrying shyness from infancy to adolescence and then into adulthood, it can develop later in life at times of transition such as coping with the end (or beginning) of significant relationships or being compelled to terminate employment.

It seems that trying to understand shyness is like approaching a chimera: the closer you get to it the more it eludes you! However, wherever the truth lies, the only thing that matters as far as you are concerned is how you can overcome your particular form of shyness. There may be some value in understanding its roots but primarily, it's about finding the key to master it in the way that brings you the greatest access to life.

Activity 1.3

The source of your shyness

Have a think about the source of your shyness:

Is shyness a trait you see in family members? *Perhaps your family tends towards social awkwardness so you haven't learned to develop more sophisticated social skills.*	
Did you feel apprehensive at school? *Shy people tend to be the target for teasing and bullying, leading to apprehension and timidity, which attracts still more teasing and bullying. Did this happen to you?*	

Were you in the midst of a social group at school or were you solitary?

Shy children are often seen on their own in the playground, finding social interaction too difficult or threatening. Perhaps this is something you can relate to.

Did you feel insecure in your attachment to your parents or carers?

Think about how secure you were as a child. Did your parents or carers make you feel 'safe' and respond appropriately to your emotional ups and downs? Were they dependable?

Were you nervy and tearful as a child?

As a shy person, your 'flight' response may have been triggered frequently, resulting in agitation and anxiety.

Did you live in a culture that celebrated the demure behaviours and chastised the bold behaviours?

Shyness can be a product of the proving ground you experienced as a child. The culture of the society you were raised in, or the family you were raised by, can condition – perhaps inhibit – the way you respond to social situations. What was your experience?

Now, think about the shy characteristics that have emerged as a result:

Do you share your inner thoughts and feelings with friends?

Shy people tend to have a few close friends with whom they share their inner thoughts rather than a large group of friends among whom they can enjoy banter and bon homie.

Do you tend towards paranoia?

As someone who is likely to live in your head, do you extrapolate experiences from the past into the future and catastrophize these? Do you have a tendency towards paranoia?

Are you socially hesitant?

Shy people tend to think twice, sometimes three times, before they interact. If they're not listing all the reasons why they hate the situation, they may be rehearsing, silently, what they're going to say so that they are not put in the position of having to improvize. Does this describe you?

Do you tend to live in your head and concern yourself with the past or the future?

Being someone who is a little withdrawn from the world, you may find yourself reflecting on things that went bad in the past and things that you dread about the future. Both these activities distract you from what's happening presently and drain your social resources. Where is your focus of attention?

Do you think about the consequences of your behaviour or build frightening scenarios?

When you venture into your head, you are quite likely to build stories around what's going on and, very often, these are vivid in their drama and large in their consequence. These stories merely create large psychological barriers over which you have to jump in order to feel in control of yourself, behaviourally speaking. How do you overcome the psychological barriers you put up?

Do you tend to have a few really good friends?

As someone who is socially hesitant, you may have built a small but trusted group of friends who understand you well and hold you safely. Large crowds may not feel safe as there are too many unknowns among the various personalities. What does your circle of friends look like?

Are you considered to be a great listener with high levels of empathy?

While you are not talking, you may well be listening acutely to others' renditions. This enables you to hear what they're saying and empathize with their positions. People may know this of you and come to you for succour when they're feeling down. In fact, if you develop a reputation for being a sympathetic ear, you may begin to feel used – in spite of feeling grateful that the focus of attention is on someone else!

Do your socially awkward memories dominate when you're anticipating a social encounter?

People who are shy usually have a battery of unfortunate experiences that they draw from when they're predicting the outcome of a social encounter or event. These times of awkwardness are brought back to haunt them and fuel their anticipation with anxiety. Is this what you do?

Do you remember people who have hostile expressions?

Because shy people notice the horrors of social interaction, they also remember the horrible people that they have encountered in a social situation. This equips them to avoid such people a second time, a talent that is not shared by the less discriminating, socially confident person. Do you recall the faces of people who have been hostile to you in the past?

What do you notice, overall, about your shyness? On the 'nature–nurture' continuum, where do you think you sit?

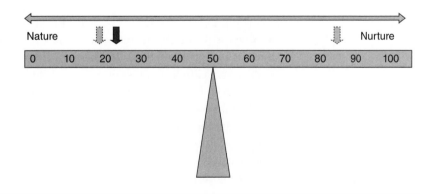

From the preceding range of opinions, from 'nature' to 'nurture' (and from your own particular manifestation of shyness), we can see that an absolute definition of shyness is impossible. However, if we acknowledge that this 'nature–nurture' continuum exists, and postulate that each end is bound to hold some truth, then we can move forward on the basis that, if we can acquire shy behaviours, then we can also 'un-acquire' them. In addition, we might also recognize that some people will have a personality predisposition that makes them susceptible to shyness, while others don't.

So, taking the view that, regardless of our genetic inheritance, there is ample potential to manage our own reactions and responses to situations, we will be working with the following four domains of shyness that are generally accepted in the literature:

▶ **Emotional/a-rational** – imagined outcomes based upon conditioned and transient responses to triggers that were laid down in your formative years. These may be *driven* by your personality type but are not facets of your personality. They may result in physical symptoms such as excitement, sweaty palms, rapid breathing or blushing.

▶ **Behavioural** – the inability to respond skilfully or adapt to meet the demands of the situation. These may be learned behaviours that 'work' as means of survival or of gaining validation. They may be underpinned by your cultural/family influences and values.

▶ **Rational/conceptual** – 'reasoned' analysis of a situation, the dominance of internal messages such as what you believe to be true of yourself, the expectations you have of yourself in different circumstances and the propensity to evaluate your successes/failures in performing to your expectations.

▶ **Situational/circumstantial** – specific, and perhaps isolated, instances such as when you are called upon to give a presentation or ask someone for a dance. Expectations in these instances may also be driven by the context, such as weddings, award ceremonies or rites of passage.

According to Dr Carducci, Professor of Psychology and Director of the Shyness Research Institute at Indiana University Southeast, most shyness is acquired through life experience but remains hidden to those on the outside. Indeed, most of us have techniques that prevent our shyness from being displayed, whether it is total withdrawal from a social situation or tools and techniques that we can adopt to help us get through the social ordeal that we're facing. The hidden nature of shyness tends to isolate us in our experiences and creates a 'conspiracy' of silence about it. Feeling that we are the only ones experiencing a debilitating response to social situations, our attention turns to 'the self'.

In his analysis, Dr Carducci suggests that shyness has three components:

- **Excessive self-consciousness** – Shy people tend to feel exposed, visible and the centre of (unwanted) attention. They feel that the full extent of their own feelings of awkwardness are visible on the outside and being judged.

- **Excessive negative self-evaluation** – Shy people tend to compare themselves negatively to everyone else. They may think that something is 'wrong' with them and this leads to them doing and saying the 'wrong' things.

- **Excessive negative self-preoccupation** – Shy people tend to be overly self-aware of themselves in everyday contexts and see themselves in a negative light.

These three components of shyness are somewhat self-oriented, yet, when compared to the negative experiences that shy people have, these connotations of self-orientation are probably the last thing on their mind! However, the proposition that shy people are overly and uncomfortably concerned about themselves may lead to some approaches that enable them to place more emphasis on the importance of others, thereby forgetting their own sense of exposure.

Where to next?

In this chapter, you have been encouraged to think about how you perceive your form of shyness and the descriptive terms (probably pejorative!) that you use to describe it. By reframing these, you are in a better position to 'befriend' some of the more positive attributes of your shyness and magnify these to your advantage.

You were given a potted view of what the psychologists and geneticists are saying about shyness. In terms of its cause, the 'nature–nurture' debate is pivotal in their speculation, yet no definitive conclusion has been reached. Most are agreed, however, that shyness is NOT a product of being an introvert and NOT all extraverts are bold. It is these types of misconceptions, however, that 'steal' the ability of individuals to express their personalities without prejudice.

You were also introduced to the four forms of shyness that are generally accepted. These help you break down the territory into 'bite-sized-chunks' so that you can get your head around them in the most efficient and effective way. Already, you should be regarding your shyness with more understanding and compassion and have gained some appreciation of what it will mean to take more control over one or more of the four dimensions – circumstantial, behavioural, emotional and rational.

In the next chapter, you will be given the chance to fill in a questionnaire. This is designed to get you thinking about the extent to which your shyness debilitates you. On the 'boldness–shyness' continuum, you are asked to position yourself so that you can see where the 'weight' of your social tendency lies. This will help you think about what you need to do to make the changes in your levels of self-assertion that you wish.

Keeping a note:	
What insights have you had as a result of reading this chapter?	
What are you going to do differently as a result of your insights?	

How shy are you?

In this chapter, you have an opportunity to respond to a questionnaire that will trigger your thinking about the form of shyness that afflicts you and the extent to which it debilitates you.

You are also asked to position yourself on the 'boldness–shyness' continuum so that you can see where you're starting from. This helps you decide what you need to do to make the changes that you wish.

Let's begin by reflecting on the extent of your shyness.

 Activity 2.1

The 'how shy' questionnaire

Respond to the statements in the following survey as honestly – and as quickly – as possible.

'Always' means that this is your default position. If you thought about it, there would be the odd occasion when 'always' wasn't true, but don't be too picky. Go with the spirit of your natural style.

'Sometimes' means that there will be occasions when the statement is true but this will not be your natural default position. It may be that there are certain circumstances that facilitate you expressing yourself and others that don't.

'Never' means that this statement does not characterize your social style at all. In fact, the opposite is generally true!

When you have answered all the questions, just summate each column and put your total in the box at the bottom of the table.

	Always	Sometimes	Never
1. When I'm at a party where I don't know many people, I like to meet as many new people as possible.			
2. When I'm due to give a presentation, I enjoy putting it together and anticipating it going well.			
3. When I like someone and want to spend more time with them, I assume they feel the same.			
4. When I'm called upon, unexpectedly, to give my view in a meeting, I rise to the challenge and enjoy sharing my opinion.			
5. When I have a difficult message to impart to someone, I feel confident and able to do so with sensitivity.			
6. I feel able to say 'No' whenever I wish.			
7. I'm able to ask for what I need or want without embarrassment or apology.			
8. When I'm in a place, circumstance or country that I am not familiar with, I get excited about what I will experience and learn.			
9. I am a confident person.			
10. When I'm invited to a surprise party, I look forward to it immensely.			
11. I am able to articulate my thoughts clearly in all circumstances.			
12. I am able to listen to others' opinions without losing my own.			
13. I am able to take responsibility for myself and not be dependent on others.			
14. When I'm asked to take on a project in an area that is unfamiliar to me, I look forward to picking up some new skills.			
15. I am able to give and receive feedback.			
16. I don't mind being different and stepping out from the crowd.			
17. I enjoy a good debate and am able to express a different opinion.			
18. I like to influence the mood of a gathering of people.			

19. When I'm invited to a formal event that is not familiar territory for me, I anticipate an exciting adventure.			
20. When an attractive stranger comes up to me and engages me in a 'pick up' conversation, I am able to rally my wits and get the outcome I want.			
21. I am good at standing up and talking to groups of people.			
22. I take the leadership role in a group.			
23. I enjoy going to new places.			
24. I am confident making formal presentations.			
25. I like ambiguous and unexpected situations.			
26. When someone in authority approaches me and I have no idea why, I assume that they are on my side.			
27. When I'd like to get to know someone more intimately, I assume that my desire will be reciprocated.			
28. When I'm invited on a blind date, I expect it will go well and, if it doesn't, I'll enjoy it anyway!			
33. I embrace the unknown without concern.			
35. New experiences are attractive to me.			
36. Difficult situations don't affect my ability to communicate.			
TOTAL			

If you answered 'always' more than 18 times, this suggests that you're bold; a pretty outgoing and confident sort of person who doesn't suffer readily from being shy. Most circumstances are manageable by you and you step into them with assurance, knowing that you can trust yourself to deal with whatever is put on your path. You may find that others, observing this, either attach to you or avoid you. They may attach to you to shield their own feelings of inadequacy and rely upon you to pave the way to their social success. They may avoid you because they feel cowed by your self-assurance and feel that they can't measure up. There will also be others who match your lack of inhibition with whom you can form relationships that keep social pace with each other.

If you answered 'sometimes' more than 18 times, this suggests that your shyness is not universal but circumstantial. There will be situations where you are confident in your ability to field the eventualities of the moment and there will be others that quell you and prevent you from putting your best foot forward. This suggests that there is more you can do to leverage your capability into the situations that you dislike or that resonate with a bad experience from your past.

If you answered 'never' more than 18 times, it would seem that you're shy and your shyness has too much control over your life and that you have not mastered your emotional susceptibilities, rather, they have mastered you. In order to be in control of your life, you need to reverse this dependency so that you can protect yourself from other people – or other situations – pulling your strings. Achieving this will enable you to realize your full potential without the usual inhibitions getting in the way. This is truly a goal worth aiming for!

If none of the categories received a score of 18, it would appear that you have a variety of resources that are transferable. You seem to use them in some situations but not in others. This suggests that, with some careful examination and planning, more of your personal resources could be made available to you more frequently.

Activity 2.2

You on the continuum of shyness

Looking at your scores above, where are you on the 'boldness–shyness' continuum and what do you want to do about it?

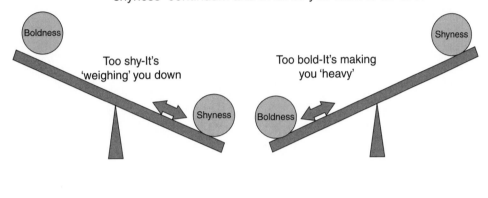

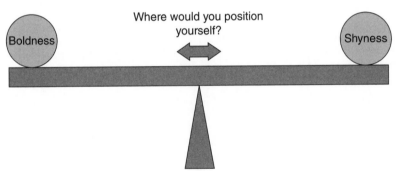

The continuum of shyness

Place an arrow on the see-saw that represents how you feel about the level of shyness or boldness that you express. If you position yourself close to the 'shyness' end, there is too much 'weight' to allow you to get off the ground. If you position yourself close to the 'boldness' end, you may be too 'heavy' and lacking the sensitivity that will enable you to interpret the appropriate response in different situations.

Ask yourself:

What are the
consequences of your
position on the shyness–
boldness continuum?

Where does your
aspiration lie in terms
of how far along the
continuum you want to
go – and how would it
change your life?

28

Where to next?

In the next chapter you are asked to reflect upon what kind of shyness you express using the four characteristic types: circumstantial, behavioural, emotional and rational. You achieve this through completing a questionnaire, which will prompt you to respond in these four domains.

In addition, you are asked to contemplate the types of circumstances in which your shyness manifests and the assumptions you hold that may get in the way of you changing your style. If you find it hard to identify your personally held assumptions, you will be asked to reflect on how you view others and the assumptions that you make about them. By doing this, you may throw light on the kind of assumptions you hold about yourself. We are often opinionated about those traits we see in others that we dislike in ourselves!

Keeping a note:	
What insights have you had as a result of reading this chapter?	

What are you going to
do differently as a result
of your insights?

3

What kind of shy are you?

In this chapter you are supported in finding the answer to the following question:

What kind of shy are you?

You access this information through a questionnaire that allows you to understand more about:

▶ In what circumstances your shyness manifests

▶ The assumptions you hold that keep you shy

And you are asked to begin to reflect upon where those assumptions came from.

To understand the nature and extent of your field of shyness, you are invited to fill in a questionnaire. It asks you to think about whether your shyness overwhelms you and gets in the way of you living your life in line with your potential or is contained and only emerges in very specific circumstances, such as when you are obliged make a presentation or speech. It helps you think about whether you are shy in one context (at work) but not in another (at home). It enables you to identify whether the values you were given as a child result in a reticence to put yourself 'out there' or forces you 'out there' to display certain behaviours that do not feel natural to you. The questionnaire also focuses upon your assumptions and psychological frames that may be challenged as you re-think your coping strategies. Indeed, the questionnaire is the first tool to help you manage your shyness in a way that puts you in control of your life; not in a 'whip cracking, harsh task-master' kind of way but in a sympathetic way that allows you to express yourself without inhibition.

The shyness questionnaire

As you respond to the questionnaire, be conscious of how you make your choices and what they are telling you. Don't think too long and hard before you make your mark on the grid below. This is a subjective instrument and will be most useful if you respond in an intuitive way.

Answer the questions by selecting a letter 'a', 'b', 'c' or 'd' that most resembles your general approach. When you have done so, on the matrix below the questionnaire, circle your chosen letter in the row corresponding to the question number.

1   When I'm at a party where I don't know many people, I:

   a Experience physical symptoms of anxiety as I try to overcome the fear that I'm going to make a fool of myself

   b Try to replicate, and learn from, the behaviours that I see around me

   c Give myself a list of reasons why I am able to deal with the event and plan my approach

   d I pick and choose the situations in which I socialize

2   When I'm due to give a presentation, I:

   a Have to deal with physical symptoms of fear before putting myself in front of the audience

   b Rehearse the presentation beforehand so that I am as near to word, and message, perfect as possible

   c Engage in self-talk to create the right mental space for me to be successful

   d Orchestrate the space and outline the etiquette I wish people to follow

3   When I like someone and want to spend more time with them, I:

   a Send out 'welcoming signals' and wait for them to approach me

   b Think through my behavioural tactics and analyse which one would be best in the circumstances

c Tell myself that any outcome is OK really but list a number of reasons that will protect me from the impact of any rejection

d Find someone with whom to create a situation that will lead to the possibility of spending more time together

4 When I'm called upon, unexpectedly, to give my view in a meeting, I:

a Feel my skin prick with sweat and my face flush before giving the minimum response

b Make sure I say something at the outset of the meeting so that my voice isn't alien to me when I have to respond to a question

c Try to remember that my experience and views are valuable, and valued, and use some delaying tactics while I gather my wits. (For instance: 'Would you say more about why you're asking this question?')

d Make sure that it's appropriate I'm at the meeting and sit in a comfortable place that allows me to participate, or not, as I wish

5 When I have a difficult message to impart to someone, I:

a Get nervous and imagine how I'll deal with the negative scenarios that will occur

b Practise giving feedback and find some phrases that will serve me in most of the eventualities

c Remind myself that I am being reasonable and that there is nothing wrong with being honest and assertive

d Make sure that I understand my rights/position so that I feel safely contained by the situation

6 When I'm in a place, circumstance or country that I am not familiar with, I:

a Keep quiet and observe what's going on so that I don't put a foot wrong

b Watch what others are doing and try doing similar things

c Test out in my mind several approaches to see which one I'm most comfortable with

d Stay close to people who are familiar and comfortable in the place and attach myself to them

7 I've been invited to a surprise party and I'm feeling shy about going so I:

   a Conjure up warm feelings for the person for whom the surprise is being planned to diminish my own self-consciousness

   b Make sure that I have a task so that I can busy myself in the kitchen

   c Tell myself to get a grip and imagine the joy that the recipient will feel when the surprise is announced

   d Make sure that I have someone to go to the party with and an excuse that will allow me to exit early if necessary

8 I've been asked to take on a project in an area that is unfamiliar to me so I:

   a Try to contain my emotions and save my panic until I'm in a safe place

   b Find someone who has run such a project before and ask if they'll coach me

   c Learn as much as possible about the project so that I understand its rationale and purpose

   d Remember that I'm capable in other circumstances and leverage those capabilities into the current one

9 I've been invited to a formal event and I've not had much experience in these types of occasions so I:

   a Try to remember the times that I have excelled in difficult circumstances

   b Read up on the etiquette of these types of events and practise with a trusted friend

   c Tell myself that we're all the same inside and that everyone will be feeling the pressure of this occasion

   d Make sure that I'm with a person or a group who have experienced this before

10 When an attractive stranger comes up to me and engages me in a 'pick up' conversation, I:

   a Get tongue-tied and can't seem to find the words I need to show my interest

   b Try to be bright and coquettish by accessing behaviours that I think will be attractive c Get into my head and try to impress the person with my attitudes, beliefs and knowledge

    d Look over my shoulder to see who they're *really* talking to and try to remove myself from the situation as soon as possible

11 When I am pulled over by the police and have no idea why, I:

    a Immediately feel guilty and wonder what I've done wrong

    b Behave in an over-obliging and deferential way to reduce the chance of any escalation

    c Go through my actions in the past few minutes to double check that I haven't done anything untoward

    d Adopt the recognized code of conduct in these situations such as remaining calm, waiting for clarification and being respectful

12 When I'd like to get to know someone more intimately, I:

    a Get nervous that I'll make a fool of myself and/or be rejected so give up before I've started

    b Look in my behavioural toolkit to see whether I've done such a thing before and whether I could tailor the approach to fit the current circumstances

    c Work out what approach I could take that would give me a credible way out if things didn't work as I wanted them to

    d Try to find a situation in which it would feel natural to get close

13 When I'm invited on a blind date, I:

    a Get really panicky and feel sick

    b I don't know what to do or say so I ask my friend how I should behave

    c Tell myself it'll be the same as always and to 'get brave'!

    d Reject the offer, politely, with some well-thought-through excuses

When you have completed the questionnaire, total each column in the matrix below, counting '1' for each letter that you circled, so that you have a score each for 'a', 'b', 'c' and 'd'.

Use the following matrix to record your responses:

Question number	'a'	'b'	'c'	'd'
1	a	b	c	d
2	a	b	c	d
3	a	b	c	d
4	a	b	c	d
5	a	b	c	d
6	a	b	c	d
7	a	b	c	d
8	a	b	c	d
9	a	b	c	d
10	a	b	c	d
11	a	b	c	d
12	a	b	c	d
13	a	b	c	d
Total				

Check your overall score against the paragraphs below. Does one of these describe you?

→ If you scored mostly in the 'a' column, your shyness type is likely to be: Emotional/a-rational

As a person whose shyness pivots, primarily, around your emotional state, you may find that you are overwhelmed by a sense of panic or inadequacy when you are in a situation, either planned or unplanned, that you feel exposes you. Your emotions may trigger physical tension such as biting down on your back teeth or bracing yourself, ready for 'fight' or 'flight'. You may literally feel tight-lipped and begin to stutter or stammer, or you may just find that you are unable to access what's going on in your mind through feelings of bewilderment and confusion. Physiological stress reactions may also emerge in the body – heart quickening, palms sweating, shallow breathing, stomach churning, face blushing...

When you reflect upon your emotional response to a situation, you may bemoan the fact that you do not show yourself as you really are; that your true personality is shielded and unable to shine through. This may be accompanied by feelings of disappointment, or even failure.

Body language falls into this category as it conveys (or betrays) what's going on inside. However skilled you are, there will be 'leakage', or signs that you are not congruent with what you're feeling. Maintaining eye contact – or not maintaining eye contact – is the most obvious give away. Looking over someone's shoulder when you're talking to them is a clear avoidance tactic, along with making yourself 'invisible' by walking 'small'; in a crouched, low energy kind of way, or backing up against the wall before leaving a difficult situation altogether.

Emotions do not stand the scrutiny of reason so however you talk to yourself, 'This is nuts. It makes no sense!', it won't change your shyness response. Unfortunately, these experiences can trigger undermining self-talk which, along with unrealistic expectations of how you 'should be', creates a vicious cycle; thoughts and feelings working against each other. (See the 'rational' shyness symptoms below.) However, all is not lost. Emotions can be mastered, and this is what the workbook will endeavour to do so that you feel more in control of how you manage your shyness.

→ If you scored mostly in the 'b' column, your shyness type is likely to be: Behavioural

If your response to being shy is behavioural, you are likely to employ strategies for dealing with your feelings of awkwardness. You may, for instance, use the bold tactic of claiming capabilities that you don't feel you have. Perhaps this is based upon the belief that you can 'Fake it until you make it!' Or you may go the other way and tell everyone 'Oh, I could never make a speech, I'm far too shy!' Alternatively, you may use displacement activities, such as washing up at a party or resorting to serving food. (Sometimes, when armed with a dish of canapés, it is easier to strike up a conversation and feel more confident.) These behavioural responses are likely to be visible enough for people to recognize them and, if they're wanting to be 'kind', they may help you by not putting you into situations that you'd find challenging or meeting those challenges on your behalf.

You may be concerned with 'acting in the right way' and spend some time and energy on researching or observing the etiquette that is considered appropriate in a particular situation. How do you behave when you go to an opera, for instance, or a concert, where the applause is reserved for specific points in the repertoire? So, in these trigger moments, those who have a behavioural response to shyness, tend to hide behind what they think is correct and mask their true feelings and inclinations. This can be a useful strategy, as long as you don't lose yourself totally in the process by building relationships based upon the behaviours that you feel are acceptable rather than the genuine expression of who you are.

So, a behavioural response to being shy is all about your skill and dexterity in dealing with a variety of different situations. No doubt you have experienced an increase in confidence as you developed your profession or expertise. It is the same with a behavioural response to being shy. You may not learn to *enjoy* taking the social initiative or take pleasure in orchestrating a social event proactively, however, these are skills that can be developed through practice and, once learned, they will serve you well.

Also, if your shyness is 'behavioural' you may find yourself being unable to express a contrary point of view, give challenging feedback or ask for something you need or would like. You may also find it difficult to say 'No!'; feeling inferior and not believing you have equal rights to someone you put in authority. At a party, you may feel unable to strike up a conversation with a stranger or take the social initiative, being aware of a general feeling of embarrassment that prevents you from being yourself.

→ If you scored mostly in the 'c' column, your shyness type is likely to be: Rational/conceptual

People who fall into this category are generally caught up in their heads with messages, usually pretty negative ones, going round and round. These thought patterns are probably irrational, but they may be based upon a seed of truth or a firmly held assumption, which makes them hard to pluck out and dispense with completely. Catastrophizing, by exaggerating the consequences of a situation, creates a large obstacle in the head to overcome. It goes a bit like this: 'If I attend this work event,

I'll make a fool of myself, and everyone will laugh at me, and my boss will think me useless, and he won't give me a promotion, and eventually I'll get fired, and I won't get another job, and I'll lose my home, and I'll end up under a bridge drinking methylated spirits!' Catastrophizing is based upon being critical of oneself with unreal consequences. As the story builds, it generates a kind of seductive hysteria that is hard to let go.

When entering a situation, people whose shyness is primarily rational/conceptual, have a tendency to do so with negative self-expectations. They judge themselves harshly, probably against a perfectionist standard, and when reviewing the situation they may say to themselves 'I've done it again!!' They may imagine that others have the 'social competence gene' that they are missing and speak of themselves in terms of generalizations and absolutes: 'I shall NEVER be able to do this!' 'I ALWAYS screw up!' – thus creating another insurmountable psychological obstacle to overcome. They are likely to be engaged in constant self-monitoring – 'I probably will never get this right!', counting the occasions that they 'get it wrong' as evidence that they'll never 'get it right'! They may also hold an internal fantasy about what it would be like if they excelled from a social perspective – thereby making it harder to do so – and they often feel that others are watching them and judging them harshly.

Those who suffer from a 'rational' form of shyness generally value their intellect and speed of intellectual processing. However, it tends to work against them as they alight upon a set of assumptions that put them at a disadvantage – and they do this with utter conviction and lightning speed. They hold an internal dialogue that enumerates the reasons for not doing something, thinking that these are all well founded and immutable. They think they know about others' motivations and capabilities, all of which are used to justify the reasons why they cannot take the initiative. It is almost impossible to argue against their analysis because they are quick witted and convinced they are working with facts. They are likely to act upon the injunctions they were given by their parents and drive for perfection in meeting them.

This constant chatter in the head is hard to silence because the elaboration is so colourful. However, with practice and discipline, it is quite possible to override the messages and change them with more helpful ones.

→ If you scored mostly in the 'd' column, your shyness type is likely to be: Circumstantial/situational

People for whom shyness is circumstantial or situational are likely to excel in one context but 'fail' in another. Some people find it easier to perform well in formal situations because the rules of engagement are clear and the protocols drive their behaviour. However, when they are 'freewheeling', they may find it harder to feel comfortable. An example might be someone who is extremely confident socially, except when they are in danger of being humiliated or rejected, such as when asking someone out on a date.

These people often follow the accepted tracks of social engagement, although they may be quite capable of commanding their own environments, which they interpret according to their understanding and belief of what is required. For instance, they may forge a new culture in a working environment or display a unique way of tackling a job. This is because the working environment justifies them imposing their expertise, strength of character and individualism. They generally understand the rhythms that drive rituals and ceremonies and are great at orchestrating events – even those that oppose the audience's expectation – as long as they don't have to put their personal frailties on the line in terms of others' acceptance or poor opinion.

The person whose shyness revolves around circumstances usually has very specific 'no go' areas that don't make much sense to bystanders who see them, in other contexts, acting with great confidence and capability. Yet they're quite susceptible to being tripped up by specific social exchanges. The role that this person carries, therefore, is quite important. But when that role is removed and the soft underbelly of their personality is exposed, they are less comfortable and may appear uncharacteristically shy.

Here are some examples of 'situational' shyness: not feeling able to ask someone to dance or go out on a date; disliking being made the centre of attention unexpectedly by, for instance, being asked to contribute to a debate with a small group of relatively unknown people or to make a speech without warning; dealing with surprises like a party or a celebration to recognize an achievement. The feature that these examples share is the risk of being publicly humiliated while the reigns of control are held elsewhere.

The questionnaire has highlighted a number of different situations in which shyness may emerge. Have a think about your responses to the questions, and the category of shyness that has emerged from them, and consider what new insights you have derived from the process.

What are the assumptions that hold you back?

What assumptions do I hold that results in my shyness?	
What expectations do I have of myself in different situations?	

*What internal messages
am I giving myself
that undermine my
confidence?*

If you have difficulty identifying your own assumptions, bring to
mind someone whose behaviours you find somewhat repellent.
This person may be overly bold, for instance. Then ask yourself the
following questions:

*What behaviours do
I see in them?*

What messages come to mind when I observe these behaviours?

What assumptions do I hold about these behaviours?

By considering behaviours that are opposite to yours, in this case, say, an overly bold person, what you will notice is the negative manifestation of a behaviour you will not allow yourself to display; a behaviour you'll withhold on the assumption that it is 'distasteful' or for which you will experience negative consequences. The reaction that someone else triggers in you is helpful in throwing light on your hidden but firmly held assumptions. In this case, you might consider such a person's behaviour as dominating, unattractive, pushy, controlling... If these are the type of descriptors you use, it will tell you something about what's in your own mindset. Here, 'boldness' gets twisted up with the behaviours that you see as negative. (Therefore, the only option is to be shy.) So, your assumption that 'bold is bad' prevents you from being bold – or even confident.

Building on the assumptions that you've identified above, see whether you can create a list that comprises the assumptions that hold you back the most. Here is a list, to which you can add, that may resonate with you. Do they keep you shy? Tick those that you need to pay attention to and add your own in the blank spaces at the foot of the table.

Assumption	✓ Put a tick against any of the assumptions you hold
Being bold is pushy	
Confident people are self-satisfied	
Bold people are egocentric	
Expressing passion is self-indulgent	
Being angry demonstrates lack of self-control	

Giving feedback is critical and unkind	
Challenging opinions is disrespectful	
Having a different opinion causes conflict	

Now ask yourself:

What do you notice about the assumptions you hold?	
Do you see a pattern emerging?	
Where did these assumptions come from?	

One of the main themes of this workbook is to develop your ability to get in control of the mindset that keeps you shy. This is the first step in fulfilling that aspiration because, once you've identified your tacit beliefs, you are half way towards getting them under your control.

For those of you who find it hard to identify your assumptions from a 'standing start', so to speak, you will be presented with some useful conceptual frames in Chapter 10 when we take a look at 'rational' shyness.

Where to next?

In this chapter, you have had an opportunity to reflect on the type of shyness that is typical of you. Through responding to the questionnaire and unearthing some of your assumptions, the expectations that you have of yourself and the pressure under which you put yourself, will be surfacing. It is worth spending some time noting what patterns are emerging from your observations and reflections and whether these give you a clue about what you could do differently. (Don't forget to note these in the 'Keeping a note' grid below.)

Next, we focus on how you are rewarded for being shy. Although this may be a counter-intuitive notion, it is certainly true that shyness has some benefits that may make it difficult to change. By taking a realistic look at the 'paybacks' you receive from being shy, you can decide whether or not you want to perpetuate this trait. (An example of a 'payback' (or a secondary gain) is: If you fight shy of making a presentation and get someone else to do it for you, your payback is that you don't have to do the work, take a personal risk or make yourself vulnerable.)

Keeping a note:	
What insights have you had as a result of reading this chapter?	

What are you going to do differently as a result of your insights?

What are the primary and secondary gains from being shy?

Some people would say that there were plenty of hidden advantages to being shy because, if there weren't, no one with a sane mind would choose to perpetuate this debilitating social condition. So, although it may appear counter-intuitive, this chapter will challenge your feelings of helplessness at your shyness and highlight some of the advantages (primary gains) and unintended benefits (secondary gains) that you may experience.

First, let's define what we mean by 'primary' and 'secondary' gains. Primary and secondary gains are terms that describe the psychological benefits of an illness or condition. In a similar way, the terms are being used here to describe the primary and secondary gains of shyness. One primary gain of shyness is that you don't have to put yourself into situations where you feel that your self-esteem would be at risk. You justify avoiding them by 'being shy' – or modest, or ego-less – and thus you are able to retain your *inner* state. (This is equivalent to not having to go to work if you are ill.) A secondary gain is having people assist you to compensate for your shyness so, not only are you able to perpetuate this trait but also, you are served or advantaged in maintaining it by those in the *external* environment. (This is equivalent to having things done for you if you were ill.)

By placing your attention on these two types of gain, you are in a better position to choose whether or not you wish to continue to benefit from being shy. Once you decide *actively* that you'd like to shed your shyness, then the practical work can begin. (This will be the focus of Part II.)

Activity 4.1

What purpose does your shyness serve?

Have a think about one or two occasions when you have felt shy and unable to project yourself fully. Rather than re-evoke the emotions, try to think of each situation from an objective standpoint, with curiosity, and examine what the 'threat' was that disabled you. Also, think about how your shyness helped or hindered you and what resulted from the event.

Describe a situation when you were struck with shyness and unable to project yourself fully	
What was the 'threat' that prevented you from being socially confident?	

What purpose did your shyness serve in this situation?	
What price do you think you paid for your inhibition? (Or, what advantage did you gain from it?)	

Let's think about your responses:

What do you notice about your responses?	

What has been revealed to you?

In what other circumstances does this pattern exert itself?

Let's build upon your answer to the final questions in the grid above and try to be more specific about the advantages of your shyness.

Activity 4.2

What advantages (primary gains) do you get from being shy?

Have a think about how people perceive you as a result of your shyness. What positive assumptions do you think they make about you and how do you gain from these? (There are a few primary gains listed to get you started.)

Primary gains	✓ Put a tick against any of the primary gains that you experience – then add some of your own
I appear more approachable because I'm not taking up too much air time or space.	
I appear thoughtful because I don't 'jump in' with an immediate response to a question or situation. I think before I act.	

I am self-sufficient; I can get on with my work without depending on others.

My shyness conveys modesty and dignity. I don't shout about my achievements and accept compliments graciously.

People see me as calm and easy to be around because I'm not (apparently) dominating or working out an agenda.

I enjoy a small number of deep friendships rather than a large number of superficial ones.

People trust me to keep their confidences because I don't talk a lot.

I am considered to be empathic and a good listener.

Having built upon this list, what do you notice?

What do you notice about this list of primary benefits? What do they say about you?		

	+ve	−ve
What of your true nature is being hidden by this list? (List the bright side (+ve) and the dark side (−ve) of your unexpressed personality.)		

Now, let's look at the secondary gains of being shy.

Activity 4.3

What are the unintended benefits (secondary gains) that you get from being shy?

Have a think about what people step in to do for you or help you with and ask yourself whether that benefit encourages you to maintain your shyness. Consider the list below as a starting point and add some of your own.

Secondary gains	✓ Put a tick against any of the secondary gains that you experience – then add some of your own
People step in to help me.	
I am excused from being sociable.	
I don't have to take responsibility for maintaining a conversation.	

I can go quiet and other people will speak to fill the gap.	
I don't have to initiate conversations. Others take responsibility for this.	
I don't have to take the lead in new projects.	
People anticipate my social anxiety and plan for my comfort.	
People make excuses for me.	

Having built upon this list, what do you notice?

What do you notice about this list of secondary gains?	
What is the 'upside' of holding on to your shyness?	
What is the 'downside' of no longer being shy?	

The point of these reflective exercises is to get you to think about what is *you* (your personality or your 'authentic self') and what is your 'chosen' behaviour (your actions and reactions). Once you can sort one from the other, you can start making active choices.

Now, a quick detour on the subject of 'choosing' your behaviour, which may seem harsh or unrealistic to you. Certainly, we may be presented with situations that are outside our control, that we don't choose. But we *are* able to decide how we are going to react or respond to them, resulting in behaviour that we do choose. So, if you were faced with heavy traffic while trying to get to a meeting on time, you wouldn't be able to alter the fact that the traffic is heavy, but you would be able to decide whether to get angry and upset or whether to switch on the radio and listen to some music until the problem passes. The result in practical terms is the same; you're late for your meeting. The result in terms of your behaviour is different. You can either arrive at your meeting overly apologetic and stressed, thereby bringing the frustration of the experience into the meeting room where it will affect others, or you can arrive at your meeting relaxed and in good condition to have a productive discussion. The choice (albeit made through hard-won self-awareness and self-discipline) is yours – and it is *active*.

'Active' choices are much more powerful than passive choices and, in the example above, the active choice was the one you made when you picked your preferred reaction *consciously* from a range of alternatives. Indeed, the power of the principle holds true even when you make a choice not to do something. For instance, because we're shy, we might feel that we cannot join a social event that is on offer in our work setting. We don't really consider our attendance an option because it would be too painful for us so we ignore the option of going and just get on with doing our own thing. This is a *passive* choice; one that is made without engaging with the possibility of making a different choice.

In this instance, it might be said that we abdicated responsibility and allowed our choice to be made by our social anxiety rather than the attractiveness or unattractiveness of the event. If we were to make this same choice actively, we would put our social anxiety to one side and think about what we might gain from attending the event and whether we could see ourselves having fun and enjoying it. For good reasons, we might conclude that actually, this event holds no interest for us, so we make the *active* choice not to go.

Making an active choice suggests that we have taken responsibility for making it rather than allowing the responsibility to migrate elsewhere; to our sense of hopelessness, for instance. In the case of making a passive choice, our locus of control is external; we are victim to circumstance. In the case of making an active choice, our locus of control is internal; we are responsible for making the choice ourselves.

Activity 4.4

Thinking about active and passive choices

Which choices below are active and which are passive?

	✓ Active	✓ Passive
I don't go to social gatherings because I am so painfully shy.		
I decided not to go to the party because I wanted to go to the theatre instead.		
I couldn't go on holiday because I had no one to go with.		

I decided to go on holiday anyway because I was interested in exploring Venice.		
I didn't volunteer to make the presentation because I was sure that I'd make a fool of myself.		
I didn't volunteer to make the presentation because I had other priorities that I wanted to focus upon.		

(Questions 2, 4 and 6 are active choices. Questions 1, 3 and 5 are passive choices.)

If we hold the key to our behaviours, why is it that we cannot change our patterns at will? Most people have tried, at some point, to overcome their habits and susceptibilities through will alone. But how successful are they? Often, after a short time, they return to their former habits because they haven't properly understood the counter-effect of the secondary gain. So, if we are trying to rid ourselves of shyness, we might think we're making an active choice to do so but find that we slip back into our old ways because we haven't thought about how to cope with losing the benefits.

Part of the problem is that we've 'trained' those in our close circle to respond to us, and support us, on the basis of our shyness. They step in and rescue us from ourselves and take responsibility for our behaviours, perhaps paving the way so that we don't have to face our behavioural deficiencies. Additionally, they may take pleasure from this. As rescuers, they feel important and valued by our inability to take charge of the social situation – and so we 'dance' together, both of us knowing the steps and staying in harmony; both of us perpetuating the co-dependency, for to change it makes the other redundant. So, we click back into our familiar patterns to avoid losing our identity.

Think of those people in your circle whose behaviour unwittingly draws you back in to the pattern that you're trying to change. What do they do to achieve that? Here's a dynamic that you might recognize: In a moment of despair, you may be tempted to make the statement: 'I'm hopeless! I can't communicate properly!' Your friend gives you a reassurance: 'No you're not. You're great!' The 'I'm hopeless!' statement triggers the desired response 'No, you're great!' Both parties are running their scripts, the 'victim' (the 'hopeless' one) and the 'rescuer' (the reassuring one) and, as long as no one changes the script, it can run and run, satisfying each person that they are fulfilling their purpose.

Activity 4.5

Is your secondary gain holding you back from not being shy?

To test this, ask yourself these questions:

Am I in a more comfortable position if I hold on to my social anxiety?	
What are the implications if I am no longer shy?	
What resources will I have to develop in myself to substitute for the assistance I've been getting in the past?	

How will my relationships be affected if I lose my dependency upon others?	
If I resolve my shyness, what will my new problem be?	
(Ironically) Does my shyness make me the centre of attention and how much do I enjoy that?	

How will I win others' friendship if I don't need them to rescue me?	
How firmly do I identify with being shy and how willing am I to shed this indentification?	
How willing am I to own the manipulative potential of my shyness?	

What do you observe about your responses to the questions, and how do you feel about them? Perhaps you have already recognized that your shyness holds a secondary gain. Perhaps this is new to you? Whichever way you have been struck, have a think about what it is you'd like to do about this. There are several options:

▶ You could do nothing and let your ageing process diminish your shyness – which it undoubtedly will do – this is a *passive* response.

▶ You could reject the idea that you have the power to change and decide to carry on doing what you've always done – this is a *complicit passive* response to doing nothing.

▶ You could take your power and decide to make some changes – perhaps one pattern at a time, to see what differences you experience and whether or not these are preferable to you – this is an *active* response leading to response-ability.

Make a commitment to yourself about what you are going to do as a result of your newest insights. Set a clearly defined goal, and timeline, and set off in the direction you wish to travel in the future. Here is a template to help you get going. (You might want to use this template again and again as you advance through the material in this workbook so photocopy a blank version that you can fill in, review and change as you go.)

Action plan
Date: SMART goal (Specific, Measurable, Achievable, Realistic, Time-bound):
The benefits to me of developing this new skill: (This will keep you motivated!)

My planned actions: *(These are the specific actions that you aim to take.)*

Key observations/insights/learning points:

Feedback: *(This can be requested from anyone that you trust who was present and witnessed your action.)*

Next steps:

Keep your action plan somewhere you can see it and review it regularly. It will keep you on track.

This chapter has been a difficult one, designed to get you to examine the causes and motivations for your shyness and really face up to your part in perpetuating this condition. By challenging your current mindset, new insights will emerge that give you more options and help you to question your usual approach. Having reflected on these, you will be in a good place to start changing the dynamic of your social behaviour and find the freedom to choose what you do and how you do it.

Where to next?

In the next chapter, you are encouraged to think about those times when shyness does not enter your social space. These are times when you are 'in your flow' and you think nothing of saying what you mean and meaning what you say. Indeed, these are the moments when you are un-self-conscious and able to focus on something that matters to you more than your fear of being exposed or humiliated. It is through reflecting on these times that you will find clues to help you in conquering your particular form of shyness.

Keeping a note:	
What insights have you had as a result of reading this chapter?	

What are you going to do differently as a result of your insights?

When am I not shy?

In this chapter, we focus on those occasions when you are not shy to see what clues they hold to you overcoming this affliction. We will do this through:

▶ Calling to mind those occasions when you have not been shy

▶ Thinking about what factors are present that release you from the grip of shyness

▶ Finding a way to achieve a state that enables you to focus on something other than your shyness

▶ Putting your shyness in a larger context so that its power over you diminishes

▶ Confining your shyness to one of the four forms (circumstantial, behavioural, emotional or rational) so that you can see how you shine in the other contexts

Let's start by bringing to mind those occasions when your shyness has not debilitated you and examine what the circumstances were and what you did.

Take a look at the four boxes below, which represent the four domains of shyness and see whether you can identify an occasion when you were fully functioning – or excelling – in one or more of them. Some examples of what excellence in these domains might look like are included, but you probably have some of your own. Don't be constrained by the examples, or by the definitions of the domains, however. (If this conceptual framework doesn't work for you, just cast your mind back to those times where you were fully functioning and fully confident; so totally immersed in a task or activity that you weren't aware of anything beyond it, including: time, yourself, other people and other demands or pressures. Write it down in any of the boxes.)

Activity 5.1

Categories of shyness

Recall and record some of the times when you were fully functioning and fully confident. Which categories of shyness do they belong to? (And later, how can you use your skill in this domain to overcome your shyness in other domains?)

Emotional – What were you doing when you lost yourself to the experience and 'forgot' to be nervous or frightened? You may have:	Behavioural – What activities were you engaged in when you forgot to be shy? You may have:
• Felt uninhibited doing something under 'public' scrutiny • Managed to avoid negative expectations about yourself • Not experienced symptoms of tension • Spoken in a relaxed way, avoiding physical tension and physiological responses • Not judged yourself harshly • Had positive feelings about yourself and pleasure in your 'performance' • Been able to speak without experiencing stomach churn or a dry mouth • Been able to speak clearly without stuttering • Stood tall and felt confident in your body • Not blushed • Not panicked when you were about to meet a commitment or attend an event	• Shared a contrary point of view • Asked for something you needed or would have liked • Stood up for someone (perhaps yourself) to someone in authority • Gone to a formal event and felt in command of your own behaviour • Spoken freely in a formal setting • Struck up a conversation with a stranger • Taken the social initiative • Given challenging feedback to someone who displeased you • Been able to say 'No!' • Made a favourable impression • Spoken boldly while making eye contact with the other • Expressed feelings – both positive and negative • Been spontaneous • Avoided avoidance behaviours – stayed 'present'

Rational – What were you doing when you managed to silence your negative self-talk. You may have:

- Done something that you'd feared for a long time
- Accepted less than the perfectionist standards that you hold
- Done something your parents wouldn't approve of
- Broken away from habitual and sabotaging thought patterns
- Silenced negative self-talk
- Avoided catastrophizing before, or postmortems after, a challenging situation
- Approached a social situation with confidence
- Celebrated success without the 'but...'
- Been receptive to compliments without looking for the counter-compliments
- Had positive thoughts and expectations about yourself
- Had certainty in your ability to succeed
- Acted unselfconsciously
- Avoided being concerned by your own or others' opinions

Situational – In what circumstances were you so competent and confident that you forgot to be shy? You may have:

- Asked someone out on a date
- Hosted a party
- Made a speech
- Helped someone who was in trouble
- Been comfortable in a room full of strangers
- Been comfortable in different cultural settings
- Initiated a conversation with a group of 5–6 people who are somewhat known to you
- Entered ambiguous situations where the terms of engagement or protocols are not clear
- Met up with a group of strangers
- Networked among a group of strangers
- Got married or cemented a partnership in front of friends and witnesses
- Defended someone who is precious to you

*Research has found that levels of shyness rise slightly when the number of people encountered falls between a high number, when they become anonymous, and a low number, when personal relationships bring comfort. Therefore, groups of 5–10 people who are only somewhat known to you are commonly the most challenging. Shyness is exacerbated if you initiate the contact, because it is exposing, and when it occurs in informal settings, where the rules of engagement or prior expectations are unknown.

 Domains of shyness

Once you have examined your answers to Activity 5.1, think about how your observations can help you overcome shyness in the domain that has the greatest propensity for your shyness.

Use the following questions to prompt your thinking and planning.

Which are the domains where I am more confident and fully functioning?	
Which domain has fewer instances of confidence (the one where I am most vulnerable to shyness)?	

What skills do I exhibit in the 'strong' domains that I can transfer and use in my more vulnerable domain?

What do I need to do to practise these skills and keep on track?

What you may notice about those times when you were fully functioning and fully confident is that when you were lost in a compelling occupation, you actually 'forgot' to be shy. You probably also lost all track of time and felt that you were operating *through* your capabilities rather than *with* them. If you have not had this experience, it might be hard to identify with the words used to describe it but imagine that you just 'knew' what to do without really thinking about it; that you became totally lost in your activity; that you felt relaxed and all your thoughts and actions just seemed to happen easily and efficiently; that you had complete confidence in your ability to reach beyond what you thought you were capable of; that you were not shy. This phenomenon is called 'flow', as defined by Mihály Csíkszentmihályi[1] in his book of the same title. 'Flow' is a time of great creativity. It feels almost effortless yet is both productive and energizing.

Regardless of your educational background, cultural influences, religious persuasion, gender and so forth, 'flow' is possible. When you are in a state of flow, you will find that you are:

▶ Not shy, having 'forgotten' about the outside world and everyone in it

▶ Calm and happy while fully occupied and working towards a goal

▶ Unfettered by time and fully present without the distraction of the past or the future

▶ Completely focused and absorbed, channelling all your energy into this one activity

▶ Creative, overcoming obstacles and constraints with inventiveness and ease; feeling part of something larger than yourself

▶ Productive, having something to show for your efforts, while feeling that it is worth doing for its own sake

▶ Exhilarated and energized by the experience

Although it is unrealistic to think that you can live in a state of 'flow' all the time, it nonetheless points towards some ideas that you could employ to reduce your levels of shyness.

Generally speaking, being shy does not factor against your chances of reaching a state of 'flow'. Indeed, if you are an introverted shy person, you may even find the state conductive to your personality because of its solitary nature. However, if you are a person whose shyness comprises a strong 'rational' component, you may have trouble switching your mind off and stopping it from presenting you with all the reasons you can't achieve your objective. But let's look at what you can do to enhance your ability to reach a state of 'flow' as a shy person.

---

1 Mihály Csíkszentmihályi is a Professor of Psychology at the Claremont Graduate University in California

Activity 5.3

Achieving a state of 'flow' – What do you love to do?

We cannot be coerced into a state of 'flow'. It is not something that can be commanded into existence from thin air. It is a state that we enter of our own volition because we love what we're doing. It occurs in areas where we have already 'put in the work' and developed the skills necessary to perform our task or deliver our creative effort. It is not an experience that can be bought like a fairground ride; it is a product of our passion, our hard work and the challenge to surpass our current level of capability. So what do you love to do and what will you choose to do to experience 'flow'?

In what area of passion and expertise would you like to reach a state of flow?	

Choose a stretching and important activity.

If you are out of your comfort zone or choosing an activity for which you haven't yet developed sufficient skills, you may not be able to achieve 'flow' – or you may choose a task that is too easy for you. To achieve flow, you need to be stretched and challenged in line with your passions and skills. So what is it that you are skilled at and would like to build upon? And what is the important goal that you'd like to achieve? Make it significant; make it life or career enhancing. It doesn't matter how big or small this is, 'flow' is not a quantitative measure.

Using your current skills and experience, what is the next step that you wish to achieve?

What level of autonomy do you enjoy?

If someone else is investing in your activity and wants to control the output, you may not have the freedom and autonomy to achieve 'flow'. In what area do you have complete autonomy to make your own judgements and use your own ingenuity?

In what place or circumstance do you have complete autonomy?

How much time do you have?

Being in a state of 'flow' is outside any notion of time so it is worth ensuring that you are unconstrained in this respect. When can you give yourself the freedom of unbounded time so that you can compete the cycle of your creative aspirations?

When is the most conducive time for me to get focused on my goal?

When is your energy level at its highest?

'Flow' does not bless the preoccupied and exhausted person. If you are seeking to experience this state, think about when you have the greatest reserve of energy. Are you a morning person or an evening person? Do you feel energized after exercise or do you like to preserve your energy by relaxing before an activity. Knowing yourself in this way allows you to select the best time for you to enter this state.

At what time of day are your energy reserves at their greatest?	

How much privacy do you have?

If you are being watched or if people are interfering with your process by suggesting ways of doing things or criticizing you for doing things in a particular way, 'flow' can be inhibited or prevented altogether. Where can you go where you will not be distracted or disturbed?

Where can you go to ensure that you are uninterrupted or undisturbed by others with a vested interest in what you are doing?

By ensuring that you have created the conditions that are conducive to achieving a state of 'flow', you will have a better chance of experiencing – and re-experiencing – this extraordinary, instinctual sensation.

For those of you who are interested in what happens to us when we are 'flowing', Mihály Csíkszentmihályi suggests that our brain function is so active at these times that we are kept out of the way, so to speak, and unable to intervene. When our nervous system is processing information at such a high rate, there is no room to interrupt the process so we step aside, losing a sense of ourselves. Some people describe themselves as having vanished or disappeared while they just watch the creative process occurring. It's as if they were the craftsman's instrument rather than the craftsman.

To achieve 'flow', you must remain focused and persistent in your activity. It may not come particularly easy to you, especially if your mind keeps entering the experience and judging your progress. Harsh judgement only serves to make you self-conscious again and 'flow' thrives on unselfconsciousness. So don't give up. Keep going until you are rewarded with a sense of self-less-ness; when you are literally out of your own way.

If you are feeling bored, apathetic or you are worrying or anxious, 'flow' will be inhibited. So, make sure that you choose something you are really passionate about.

This chapter has focused on those moments when you are not shy. It may be that your shyness is confined to one of the four domains – circumstantial, behavioural, emotional or rational – in which case, there are three other domains from which you can transfer the tools and techniques that work for you.

'Flow' is a state that inhibits shyness. It is where you are so intensely focused on an activity that you love that your self-consciousness doesn't stand a chance and you can lose yourself to your activity. This was to underline the fact that by focusing on something outside yourself, you can overcome your shyness.

Where to next?

Most of us have a series of sabotaging messages, scripts or crumple buttons that go round and round. These can get so magnified that we can't imagine being free to make our own behavioural choices. Generally, these echo from our childhoods into our adult world, triggering the same child-like responses. In the next chapter, we will look more closely at these messages and the impossibility of resolving them to anyone's satisfaction; conundrums that rock back and forth fruitlessly.

Keeping a note:

What insights have you had as a result of reading this chapter?	

What are you going to do differently as a result of your insights?

6 What triggers my shyness?

This chapter will focus upon those instances that see your confidence draining away as your shyness kicks in. Sometimes as the experience is unfolding (in what seems like slow motion), the critical messages that we pass ourselves become so overwhelming that we can't recover our social abilities (and then we criticize ourselves some more just for good measure!). Generally, the triggers are internal; messages or scripts that we hold in our heads, most likely seeded in our childhood.

So, in the next few pages you will focus on your mindset and:

▶ Identify the messages you hold in your head

▶ Find the source of those messages

▶ See how the messages fit into the metaphor or story you live by

It is common for most people to have experienced moments of shyness, yet there are those for whom shyness is seriously (and visibly) debilitating. Western researchers tend to agree that this is about 20 per cent of the population. This proportion rises to between 40 per cent and 50 per cent when those who suffer their shyness in silence, are added. Mostly, these people believe that they are stuck with their shyness and they just have to get on with life the best they can. However, the good news is that shyness is not a disease, nor is it a condition over which we have no control. It is a mindset, born of individual experiences in the past and the thinking patterns and conditioned responses that emerge from these. It is here, in the mind, that the secret of change lies.

Let's look for a moment at where the messages came from that hold you in the thrall of your shyness. Cast your mind back and re-imagine what it was that you were told as a child about your social behaviour. What were the social 'imperatives' and what were the social 'limitations' that you were given? Here are some to get you into your flow. Add those that you have carried forward from your childhood to your adulthood; those that still pull your strings.

Activity 6.1

 What messages were you given as a child?

Imperatives	Limitations
Be polite and charming.	Children should be seen and not heard!
Make us proud. Show us what you can do.	Pride comes before a fall!
Have a little self-respect!	Who do you think you are?!
Think for yourself.	Respect your elders and betters!
Don't hide your light under a bushel.	Don't show off!
Show your best side.	Don't be so pleased with yourself!
Don't be boring. Engage in stimulating conversation.	Don't bore people and dominate the conversation.
Don't be selfish. Share your good fortune.	Don't be a fool and cast your pearls before swine!

Not only are we given very strong injunctions as a child, along with reward and punishment to keep us on the straight and narrow, but also they are often contradictory, thereby narrowing the social options available to us and compelling us to ricochet between one extreme and the other. Perhaps those of us who are shy are just oscillating at the midpoint of a dichotomy, uncertain which way to turn. Maybe we find it easier to stay stuck in our shyness than to challenge the wisdom of the messages we were given as children, for to challenge an insistent parent (even if that parent resides in the past) runs the risk their displeasure, or even wrath!

However, is it time to review these messages to see which ones you'd like to retain and which ones you'd like to discard? By bringing them to mind, you can make this choice actively, which is half the battle won.

It sounds simple, doesn't it, to discard the messages that are not serving you just by making your choices consciously. And on one level, it is simple, it's just not that easy!

So, let's look at a way that might help you access what's in your mind. Most of us have beliefs about how we should live our lives; frames that we see our lives through. These might form a complex storyline, a set of expectations and rules, an archetypical role, a motto or a metaphor. This psychological structure guides our thoughts, actions and behaviours; it helps us make sense of our lives and create meaning. By unearthing these structures and making them explicit, you have the chance to rework them and shape them in a way that helps you rather than hinders you.

In their book *Metaphors We Live By*, George Lakoff and Mark Johnson propose that 'Metaphor is pervasive in everyday life, not just language but in thought and action' (2003: 3). This suggests that unconsciously we enact the metaphors we hold in our heads so, if we believe, albeit unconsciously, that 'Life is an uphill struggle', we will not only notice the strenuous aspects of our lives but we will find that we have 'created' situations in which a strenuous response is appropriate in order to live congruently with our metaphor and therefore, prove it to be correct. We do this because we know who we are when our lives are aligned with our metaphor.

You may have a natural reaction against the notion that we 'create' situations that we find challenging or unpleasant but there are several arguments to suggest that this is the case. When we have an *expectation*, all our observations, decisions and actions are aligned to that expectation. Metaphorically speaking, it's a bit like using a torch to search for your lost cat in the dark. As you move the beam across the garden, you dismiss all the information that is not cat-shaped in your pursuit of some that is. In this way, you're unlikely to notice spurious information that may be important, like an open gate or a hole in the fence. Metaphorically speaking, it's the same with our expectations. If our observations, decisions and actions are like the beam of a torch, you can, perhaps, imagine that their main focus will be on fulfilling your expectation, and their job is to illuminate it and bring it to life. Hence, we tend to get what we expect. We fulfil our own prophecies. This implies that if you change your expectations – genuinely, not just as a sop to the process – you change the outcomes that you get.

In the next activity, you're going to be asked to identify your life metaphor. This is the first step to illuminating the hidden yet complex fabric of expectations that shape your life and the consequences of carrying it. This is being done in the eventual hope that you can change what you don't like and keep what you do like.

Activity 6.2

What is your life metaphor?

Metaphor	Expressions that 'betray' the metaphor	Behavioural implications
Life is a waiting game	Everything comes to those who wait.	You take a step back and wait for things to happen.
	Patience is a virtue.	You look for the reward for your patience.
	Your efforts will be rewarded.	You wait for someone to notice that you've made a contribution.
Time is short	Hurry up!	You're always rushing and trying to achieve new things.
	Don't waste your efforts.	You try to cram as much as you can into your day.
	It'll be over before you know it!	You may panic when you get delayed.
Life is a series of mountain climbs	You have more peaks to scale.	You never feel satisfied with your achievements.
	Keep putting one foot in front of the other.	You keep going even when you're exhausted.
	Don't give up!	You set yourself ambitious goals and expend huge effort reaching them.

Life is a roller-coaster	The ups are followed by the downs! When you're down, the only way is up. The faster you go, the more thrilling the ride.	You are exhilarated by the ups and discontented when down. You might appear moody and inconsistent. You may change your mind in pursuit of the ups.
✍	✍	✍
✍	✍	✍
✍	✍	✍

What triggers my shyness? **99**

Equally, we might be living out a role from a myth or fairytale that was influential in our childhood: *Cinderella, Dick Whittington and his Cat, Goldilocks and the Three Bears* or *Jack and the Beanstalk*. Or an archetype: the heroine/hero, the warrior, the caregiver or the explorer, among many others. As with the life metaphor, these structures offer us a way to make sense of our lives; informing us what to choose and providing us with the bricks and mortar that enable us to construct the blueprint of our life. And, as we have already noted, this happens out of consciousness so we carry the internal map without really noticing it; until we get feedback or reflect on our patterns for some reason.

If the notion of a fairytale is more evocative for you, have a go at identifying which one you're living and what the implications are of carrying it as a life recipe.

 What is your myth or fairytale?

Myth or fairytale	Expressions that 'betray' the myth or fairytale	Behavioural implications
Cinderella	Do as you would be done by. Good things will happen if you're uncomplaining and dutiful. You will be rewarded if you tow the line, however unfair. Forgiveness sets you free.	You work hard waiting for your reward. You fantasize about being rescued. You may get indignant when your contribution isn't recognized or appreciated. You don't hold grudges because natural justice will prevail.
Dick Whittington and his Cat	From humble beginnings, great fortunes can be won. You can overcome early setbacks. Be kind and generous and your efforts will be rewarded. Invest in others' talents and benefit from their efforts (the cat).	You are persistent and bounce back from misfortune with high expectations. You may diminish the severity of a situation or brush concerns under the carpet. You are extremely ambitious and don't take account of the setbacks. You have a false sense of your own potential. You use others' skills and capabilities.

Goldilocks and the Three Bears	'Fools rush in where angels fear to tread' – don't go to unfamiliar places or try out anything new.	You hesitate before adventuring away from home.
	Girls are the fairer sex – stay at home and be safe!	Something 'bad' will happen if you leave your familiar environment.
	Curiosity killed the cat!	You refrain from trying out anything new because it's bound be scary!
Jack and the Beanstalk	Take a chance despite the odds.	You may rush into situations.
	He who dares wins.	The end justifies the means – you may take undue chances in order to get what you want.
	Face your demons – giants – despite your size.	You may have feelings of invincibility so make rash and risky decisions.
	Use your own initiative, don't be swayed by others' advice.	You may land on your feet whatever the ungainliness of your efforts.

Does this all feel a bit too much to deal with? Does it feel that you are unable to make the choices that will fulfil your highest ambitions because there's too much 'stuff' getting in the way? If you feel like this, you may be baulking against taking responsibility for orchestrating your destiny, for that's what you're doing when you take charge of your mindset and orientate it to your highest aspirations. However, let's look at the counter argument. If you continue to let your strings be pulled by patterns out of consciousness, you'll continue to fall into those places that are uncomfortable for you and that compel you to think that you have no control over your responses; you'll be living a 'smaller' story.

So, if you were to write your own story, what would it be? Use your metaphor, fairytale or whatever other blueprint you hold in your mind and re-write it with the 'ideal' in mind. Give yourself a rich (and positive) narrative and include an amazing ending – which, of course, is also the beginning; the beginning of stepping along your life path in a way that you desire and that furnishes you with the qualities and capabilities that allow you to be the success that you want to be, whatever that is.

 **Activity 6.4**

 What's my story?

Once upon a time...

Activity 6.5

My future me

You could also write to yourself from the future. This is a good way of turning your attention to the person you wish to become. By lodging this image in your mind, you are programming it to live a different story, replete with different intentions, possibilities and expectations. Write to yourself in the first person, such as: 'It is my milestone birthday and I'm loving my life. I am enjoying the kind of success I've always dreamed of and these are the things I've done and the capabilities I've developed that got me here. I am known to be ...' Be bold in what you claim for yourself, make sure that it satisfies your highest aspirations in every dimension of your life. Go for gold!

You might like to use a website called www.futureme.org, which enables you to send yourself an email on a date in the future of your choice; perhaps two or three years from now. Have a go and see what you can manifest for yourself.

Where to next?

We've spent Part I of this workbook focusing on the shyness landscape and trying to identify what kind of shyness you suffer from and where the keys to overcoming it may lie. Now we're going to move on to the more practical business of developing the skills you need to resource yourself as you change your automatic responses to situations and people.

In Part II, you find a series of stories from individuals who have been shy and who have developed strategies for overcoming it. You are bound to find some stories that resonate with you so pay attention to these and mine them for information, thoughts and ideas that you can apply to yourself. You are asked to imagine yourself in the storytellers' shoes so that you can compare your response to theirs and then you're given their solution to add to your own and inspire some additional options.

The next chapter deals with how to cope with specific occasions that evoke a shyness response such as:

▶ Making presentations or giving a performance

▶ Dealing with interviews or socially charged situations (where you are at risk of rejection)

Keeping a note:		
What insights have you had as a result of reading this chapter?		

What are you going to
do differently as a result
of your insights?

Part II

Getting practical about developing the skills to overcome shyness

How to deal with circumstantial shyness

Having scoped the territory of shyness in Part I, this part of the workbook will be focused on the practicalities of dealing with shyness. In this chapter, you will be invited into difficult circumstances to think about what strategies you might invent to help you deal with them in a different way. This will include:

▶ Making presentations or giving a performance

▶ Dealing with interviews or socially charged situations (where you are at risk of rejection)

In many instances, the material is presented to you in the form of a story, told by someone (a 'real' person!) who has experienced the situation being described. The context in which shyness was experienced is first described. Then, you're asked to imagine yourself in the same situation and think through what you might have done in the same circumstances. This will be followed by the storyteller's response and the lessons that may be learned from this, some of which you may like to adopt for yourself.

→ Circumstantial/situational shyness

You may remember that circumstantial or situational shyness comprises specific, and perhaps isolated, instances such as when you are called upon to give a presentation, be interviewed, engage in professional networking or ask someone for a dance. Some researchers suggest that the more complex and uncertain the situation is, and the fewer rules of engagement there are to guide social behaviours, the more challenging is the situation to shy people. It is on these occasions that shy individuals are most exposed and their behaviours most indicative of their social confidence and capability. On the other hand, at events like award ceremonies, weddings or other rites of passage, behaviours tend to be 'scripted' and driven by the protocols of the occasion, along with the accepted form of etiquette. Although it is quite possible to be shy at these more orchestrated events, the structure and certainty of them can help a shy person negotiate the territory with greater dexterity.

→ Rose's story – Making a presentation

'This happened a lot at the beginning of my managerial career. One aspect of my job involved me in introducing guest speakers to groups of senior people who were affiliates of the organization I represented. I had no experience of doing this so I wasn't prepared for my reaction to standing up and speaking in public.

As a representative, my manner and style would be considered the embodiment of the organization so I was highly visible and scrutinized constantly for the way I upheld its values and mirrored its ethos. I felt as though I was being judged all the time. Actually, I *was* being judged all the time! The affiliates, who comprised the organization, sought the latest information, professional development and advice from the various departments within it. So, it was pretty high profile and important to get things 'right'.

The settings in which I made these presentations were fairly formal. Affiliates were leaders in large, multinational organizations, prestigious consultancies or the professions so it was all fairly daunting. Anyway, I put on a suit, took a deep breath and launched into my material as if on attack! As soon as I had made the introduction, I sat down to allow the proceedings free reign as discussions took place and views were exchanged. Mercifully, once this stage had been reached, my duties had been discharged for the time being. And thank goodness that was the case for, by now, I was deaf. The ringing in my ears was so loud that I couldn't have heard a thing, let alone a comment or question directed at me. This went on for many minutes until my breathing calmed and my panic receded.'

Activity 7.1

What would you advise?

So, if you were to advise Rose how to overcome her acute shyness, what would you say to her? What could she have done *before*, *during* and *after* the event that would have enabled her to stand in front of such a group with natural ease and confidence? Capture your thoughts in the following table with a view to giving Rose some helpful tips.

Before	
During	
After	

Rose's story is typical of someone whose shyness is circumstantial. In fact, she is quite confident in other areas. She graduated from university and has developed her own professional expertise. Indeed, she is successful in her field and often sought for advice and guidance. She has a good circle of friends and is not considered to be lacking in confidence. What happened to make her shy in these particular circumstances?

Delving into her story a little further, it turns out that Rose had an experience in her childhood that she feels triggered her shyness in front of an audience.

As a child, she was part of a ballet troupe and, at the end of the year, this ballet troupe put on a performance for the parents. There were many dances in the show so different groups of children would enter and leave the stage in quick succession. On this occasion, Rose was the last in her group to leave the stage but, as she was about to exit, the dance teacher stepped forward and blocked her path. She put a hoop of flowers in her hands and said 'Go back and introduce the next dance.' Shocked at this unexpected turn of events, Rose said 'No!' The teacher insisted and raised her voice a little. Rose matched the increase in volume as she protested; 'No! I don't want to!' The parents, being aware of the kerfuffle, turned to watch what was going on. The teacher won, of course, and Rose stamped her way back onto the stage and begrudgingly shouted the title of the next dance. Then she stamped back off the stage – to peals of laughter from the parents. Her horror of performance was thus seeded and, every time she returned to face an audience, the whole embarrassing episode came back to her with force.

So, what did she do?

Before	
	Attended a presentation course
	Prepared, prepared and prepared her material and notes
	Practised in front of friends in whom she had faith
	Watched others giving presentations to see what they did
	Took every opportunity to stand up in front of a group or contribute to group discussions
	Focused on her body language and how she could adjust this to make her feel more secure
	Learned about breathing and developed the ability to control this
	Visualized being superb
	Reframed her experience as a child
	Asked for observation and feedback from trusted sources

During	
	Ensured that her delivery was slowed down so that she could breathe more easily
	Instead of leaning against a piece of furniture, stood firmly on both feet to steady and stabilize herself physically
	Looked at individuals in the audience and made eye contact with the 'friendly' ones
	Spoke to the back of the room to ensure her voice was heard by everyone
	Had a glass of water handy in case her mouth dried up. (She didn't use it though!)
	Had notes available in case she forgot what she wanted to say. (Electronic presentations **can** act as a useful prompt – but use these thoughtfully.)
	Shared the platform with a colleague or co-presenter
	If she felt nervous, focused on a larger context; something that carried more importance than the presentation like a visit to her family, a holiday or a celebration of achievement
	Paused and allowed silences while she collected her thoughts
	Wore red underwear
After	
	Made sure she was available for questions/comments after the session had ended
	Thought about who in the room she should connect with and went to greet them
	Reflected on the session and recalled what went well
	Reflected on the session and recalled what didn't go so well
	Reviewed the material she delivered to make sure that she had covered everything
	Recalled the questions that were asked to see whether they suggested anything else she should include in her presentation next time
	Made notes to capture her thoughts about what needed to be changed or updated
	Asked for feedback from certain members of the audience
	Did something lovely for herself
	Followed up with certain people by email or telephone

Activity 7.2

 Capturing the learning points

How do your answers compare with Rose's?	
What new ideas have you taken away that you could try for yourself?	

Here's another circumstantial scenario.

→ Isaac's story – Asking someone to dance at a club

'I've always been shy when approaching girls so I get really nervous about doing so. Typically, this would be at a bar or in a club. If I'm approaching a girl as a friend, it's no problem, but if I find her attractive and have an interest in her as a girlfriend, I'm extremely shy. In fact, the more attractive she is, the shyer I am!

There is someone at the moment that I'd like to get close to but I'm really scared she'll reject me. Strangely, her name is Hope! We're going to be at the same club together soon but I'm not sure how it's going to go. I do have a strategy, which I've tried out before. We'll see if it works on her!'

Activity 7.3

What would you advise?

What would you recommend Isaac do *before*, *during* and *after* asking Hope to dance? Capture your thoughts in the table below with a view to giving Isaac some helpful tips.

Before	

During

After

Like Rose's story, Isaacs's is also circumstantial. Mostly, he's a confident guy, although he's still quite young. He's tall, good looking and is at the beginning of what is likely to be a prestigious career. However, he is pretty certain he knows where his shyness came from. When he was 13, he wrote a love poem to a girl he fancied. But, instead of it being the start of a beautiful relationship, it was the seed of his shyness around girls. Unfortunately for Isaac, she didn't feel as he did so she circulated the poem to everyone in his class and he became a laughing stock.

So, what did he do?

Before	
	Did his research on who her friends were, what she liked and whether or not she was available
	Made sure that she was going to be at the club on the night he was planning to be there
	Made sure that he felt good in his clothes and in his personal care
	Went through the scenario in his head to ensure that he had rehearsed all eventualities
	Tried out the words he was going to use and made sure that he felt comfortable saying them
	Confided in a trusted friend so that he had some support
	Devised a strategy* to save face should she rebuke him
	Created a contingency plan – he had his trusted friend standing by with a drink so he had somewhere to go and someone to talk to
	Made sure that he had sufficient cash to buy her a drink
	Decided to go for it!
During	
	Looked out for her in the bar
	Made initial eye contact to see if there was any obvious 'go'/'no go' signal
	Gained a bit of confidence by talking to some female friends so that she could see I was OK
	Noticed that she was with a friend and thought it might be hard to separate them so persuaded my friend to agree to dance with her friend
	Went to say hello to them both and asked her friend if she would like to dance with my friend. He stayed at the bar while I did this. (I was now the messenger so wouldn't feel rejected if the friend said no!)
	Her friend said she was worried about leaving Hope alone, so I reassured her that I would stay with her until she came back
	Signalled to my friend and he came across to take Hope's friend onto the dance floor
	After a while, asked her if she'd like to dance too
	She said yes.
	We danced!

After

Made sure I had her mobile number

Sent her a note to say thanks for a lovely evening

Asked when she was next going to the club

Suggested we meet there with our friends to make up a foursome

Began to spend more time with her on her own

Asked her out on a 'proper' date

Bought her a small gift to show her I was thinking about her

Made sure that I stayed in touch and honoured my promises

And so it went on

Hope is my girlfriend now

*The strategy that Isaac devised to protect himself from being hurt by rejection is what he calls putting on a 'sacrificial layer', a term borrowed from material science to describe a protective layer that can be destroyed leaving the precious material beneath intact. He uses this metaphor to describe the way he protects his ego by using bravado. By poking fun at himself, he avoids the impact of anyone else poking fun at him, thereby protecting his ego. (Isaac did acknowledge that by repeatedly using bravado as the disposable part of his ego, he might get a reputation for being a fool, rendering the strategy self-defeating.) In the story above, Isaac's friend helped him create a different 'sacrificial layer' by promising him social protection – companionship and a drink at the bar – if he was rejected.

Activity 7.4

Capturing the learning points

How do your answers compare with Isaac's?	

What new ideas have you taken away that you could try for yourself?

Both these stories are situation specific; situations that carry a higher risk of exposure and humiliation.

Being interviewed is another situation that renders some people inhibited and unable to show themselves in a good light. Extrapolating from the stories in this chapter, imagine that you're about to be interviewed for a job you'd really like to be given. You have all the qualifications necessary to ensure that you'd be able to do the job and your experience is relevant. This is a step up for you but you're sure that you can make the grade.

Activity 7.5

What elements can you use to help you in your interview?

Before	
	Do your research. Find out as much as you can about the organization in which you're applying for a job. (If it's appropriate, you might pen a short document that shows how you would tackle the role and the priorities that you would have.)
	Review your network to see whether you have anyone in it who can give you inside information or an introduction to someone who knows the organization well.
	Find a trusted friend or colleague to give you feedback about how you come across.
	Ask them to rehearse difficult questions with you. These might include some of the classics such as:
	What have been your most rewarding achievements?
	What have been your greatest disappointments and what did you learn from these?
	How would your colleagues describe you?
	What are your development needs?
	What are your career aspirations in five or ten years?
	Ask them to ask you 'curve ball' questions such as: 'What legacy do you want to leave the world?' or 'If you were to win the lottery, how would you spend the money?'
	Have a think about the culture of the organization and consider what would be the best clothing to suggest a fit.
	Prepare a few questions to ask your interviewer at the end of the interview.

	Think about the strengths you want them to know about and practise declaring them. You can do this with a friend or in front of a mirror. Get used to how it sounds so you don't sound alien to yourself at the interview.
	Prepare some 'small talk'. There may be some unstructured time before or after the interview. If you can link it to a relevant fact about the role or organization, so much the better.
	Think positively about yourself. Negativity 'leaks'!
During	
	If you're not sure what they're driving at, ask them to be more specific.
	Speak about your strengths and your former successes.
	Sit upright and demonstrate attentiveness. Make sure that you establish and maintain eye contact.
	If you don't feel that you've been asked the questions that show you in a good light, ask whether the interviewer would like to know more about... Be yourself. Don't try to evoke the characteristics of an incredibly confident person unless that's how you feel.
	Don't be afraid to show your enthusiasm when you're talking about something you feel strongly about.
	Be genuinely curious about the role you're applying for and the organization's culture and goals. If you're really interested and wanting to know more, you'll be less self-conscious and less shy.
	If you start feeling anxious during the interview, remind yourself that there is a bigger world out there and remember some of the nice things you have planned. Don't go off into a dream world but use these thoughts as a reality check to get things in proportion.
	'Act as if you have the role already. This is not about pretence but it does enable you to envisage the role and conjure up compatible questions and behaviours.
	Breathe and speak slowly.

After		*Immediately afterwards, write to thank the interviewers for the time they have given you.* *Let your referees know that they might be hearing from your prospective employer.* *Thank anyone who has helped you along the way – regardless of the outcome.* *Ask for feedback on how you came across and whether there were any aspects of your interview that you could have done differently.* *Review your materials to ensure that they're up to date and remedy any omissions that have emerged during the interview process.* *Send any follow-up information that's been requested promptly.*
		If you haven't heard the outcome of your interview by the agreed date, make contact to show that you're serious and still thinking about the role. *If, by chance, you are not deemed suitable for the job, accept the rejection with grace. You never know when you'll renew these acquaintances – or be recommended for another opportunity.* *You may consider inviting your interviewer to connect with you on LinkedIn.* *Thank your referees for their support and assistance.*

Where to next?

To continue the practical theme, Chapter 8 is going to focus on the behavioural type of shyness. This form of shyness results in someone withholding themselves from a social perspective. This may be such as avoiding instigating a conversation with someone they don't know, being reluctant to complain about a service or ask for something that they need. Feeling unable to impose their will, even if this were to be diplomatic and reasonable, they will likely escape into 'avoidance behaviours' to take the challenge off their plate. Following on from this, someone who is shy in this domain is also unable to say 'No' to requests, not wishing to ruffle any feathers and get themselves into situations they fear they cannot deal with. This makes them prey to 'users' who rely upon their social anxiety to succumb to their (sometimes unreasonable) requests. Of course, not all these factors need be present in one person. You may find yourself relating to elements of this description rather than the entire of it!

To help you in your behavioural shyness, you will be encouraged to adopt a helpful questioning approach, build a range of adaptive behaviours and command your body language so that you feel 'in control' of the interaction. Specifically, this chapter will include:

- ▶ Managing one's body
- ▶ Placing attention beyond oneself to 'forget' shyness
- ▶ Listening with curiosity and asking great questions
- ▶ Understanding spatial etiquette

What insights have you had as a
result of reading this chapter?

What are you going to do differently as a result of your insights?

How to deal with behavioural shyness

In the previous chapter, we looked at the specific case of circumstantial shyness. This is when shyness is confined to specific situations; those that are reminiscent of experiences in the past. Once triggered, the original reactions and responses come rushing back to re-impose themselves, stealing away any other options in the moment. Through the accounts of people who are afflicted by circumstantial shyness, practical tools and techniques were identified and offered as possible solutions.

To continue the practical theme, this chapter is going to focus on the behavioural type of shyness. This is a form of shyness that casts a pall over the shy person's social interactions and inhibits an easy flow. It also conjures up 'avoidance strategies' that allow the person displaying behavioural shyness to avoid being put on the spot and having to deal with situations they feel unable to rise to. Believing that they are unable to command their own social domain, they may be taken advantage of by those who have more guile and are on the lookout for a 'main chance'.

Again, through the experiences of others, you will be offered strategies that may help you find a different way of coping and building a robust set of tools that will give you a sense of proficiency. In particular, you will learn how to:

▶ Manage your body language – including eye contact and the quality of voice

▶ Listen to others

▶ Be fully present in the situation you find yourself in and have access to your behavioural tools and techniques to hold you there safely

→ Behavioural shyness

Behavioural shyness is broadly described as the inability to respond skilfully or adapt to meet the demands of the situation. It results in a lack of agency and manifests as social clumsiness, embarrassment, poor body language – including not being able to look people in the eye – and a quiet, uncertain or shaking voice. These may be learned behaviours that mimic those that were apparent in the family or formative setting. Indeed, they may have been underpinned by your cultural/family influences and values. But the manifestation of these once-useful social codes may not be serving you now that you are living your own life in a bigger world than the one you grew up in.

We will start the exploration of behavioural shyness by hearing the story of a young woman who was rendered helpless in social situations.

→ Elizabeth's story – Shy behaviours got in the way of my success

'I don't know where my shyness came from. I can't remember a traumatic incident when I was a child but my family was quite reserved and my mother certainly preferred to stay home with those close to her than go out to parties or anything like that. Whatever its source, I do know that being shy dogged my youth and made it impossible for me to be as successful as I would have liked to have been.

Whenever I met someone I didn't know, I would look anywhere but at them. I could feel my whole body fidgeting and I did everything I could just to stay put. The more aware of my behaviour I became, the worse it got. I blushed like a beetroot and felt really hot and sweaty. I was sure that all anyone would see was this sweating, red-faced fool with whom they'd rather not interact.

I'm an intelligent person but every time I opened my mouth, I felt that I proved myself to be foolish. I wanted to finish the conversation quickly so I'd speak really fast and my eyes would dart about all over the place. I couldn't access my thoughts so what I did say, didn't really make sense and wasn't really what I wanted to say. So, I'd say something and then smirk, or giggle. Afterwards, I could imagine what I should have said and how I could have been witty, amusing, intelligent… whatever. It was horrible. I just couldn't stop it.

It became worse when my friends started to laugh at me and say 'Oh look! You're blushing!!!' I felt really exposed and horribly aware that others could see my deficiencies. So, I began to isolate myself and avoid socializing if I possibly could. I worked hard. Got my degree. Got a job. But I was quite depressed, feeling that I'd never find a place in the world.

The worst thing was having to attend social events for my work. Occasionally, I would be placed next to a client for dinner and I'd be trapped, trying to have a conversation with someone who didn't know me, didn't want to know me and didn't follow the most basic of social etiquettes, like asking me a question! I remember one instance when I was placed on the 'top table', next to a key client. I was a budding Client Director and my boss thought it would be a good experience for me to strike up a conversation with someone who was 'on side', as it were. Well, it was a nightmare. I brightly asked how long he'd been a client of the firm that I was working for – I don't know why I did this because I knew the answer. I was panicking though, trying to find a point of convergence for our conversation. Anyway, he was clearly offended and replied that he was surprised that I was not familiar with his history. My boss shot me a look around the back of this important guest and mouthed something like 'What the f*** are you doing?!' I tried again. 'How do you feel about your current campaign?' The prized client gave me a withering look and said, 'Fine. But I'd rather talk to your colleague about that.' I said that I'd orchestrate a change of seats, and that's what I did. When the exchange took place, I disappeared. I was miserable. It was hell!'

This is a classic example of behavioural shyness. The situation pulls unhelpful behaviours from the shy person, rendering them inept and inadequate. What can also happen is a fit of stammering, the inability to initiate a conversation – or inventive avoidance strategies. What's worse, after another failed attempt at being socially ept, a shy person feels guilty or beats themselves up for not being able to cope better.

Activity 8.1

  What would you do if you were in Elizabeth's situation?

Before	
During	
After	

There are several actions you can take when dealing with this form of shyness. Some of them concentrate on what you do with your body. Others focus on your behaviours. Let's start with the body.

When you are desperately trying to avoid feeling shy, your body 'leaks' energy and looks fidgety, uncomfortable and incongruent. The most telling portrayal that gives away your shyness is the lack of eye contact. This is the most bond-breaking activity you can engage in so this is where the discipline should start.

Activity 8.2

Focusing on the other's eyes

Try focusing on the other's eyes. You can play a game with yourself to keep your attention pinned. Ask yourself:

▶ **What colour are their eyes?**

▶ **Are there any idiosyncrasies or inconsistencies in the colour?**

▶ **Is there a mood being conveyed by their eyes?**

▶ **Do you get a sense of them or are they hidden behind their eyes?**

▶ **How often do they blink?**

▶ **What is the rhythm of 'gaze'/'disconnect gaze' that works best for you both?**

Be curious about the eyes of the person you are talking to so that you remain connected. Keep in mind a note of caution, however. Gaze (the technical term for looking into someone's eyes) can be overpowering if it is maintained for too long. When you are listening, you can 'gaze' for 90–100 per cent of the time. When you are talking, you can 'gaze' for about 10–20 per cent of the time. Mostly, the talkers' eyes are glancing around looking for inspiration, recalling and visualizing situations and breaking the potential relentlessness of the stare. If you do this as a listener, the talker will soon feel unheard and their conversation will start trailing off.

Activity 8.3

Take your colour from them

When you're having a good conversation with someone, notice how your body takes on the same posture as theirs. Have a look at intimate couples dining or drinking together. You probably notice that they mirror each other physically as well as drinking or eating at the same rate. This is a natural indicator of good rapport. Knowing this, you can lead the way into good rapport by reflecting back the physical shape and demeanour of your conversational counterpart. When we are shy, we might do anything but mirror the other as we physically shrink away from them both emotionally and physically.

Be conscious of the space between you too. You will probably be able to sense the 'right' distance. Too close and it feels like an intrusion. Too far away, and it feels like a disconnection. This will be dependent upon the type of relationship you have with the person you're engaging with and the space will be determined by mutual consent – in an ideal world!

The different levels of social distance between two people are illustrated below. The densely coloured overlap denotes two people at 'social distance'.

This is what the different distances mean:

▶ The intimate distance is appropriate for those who are in a close relationship.
▶ The personal distance is appropriate for two people who are in conversation with each other.
▶ The social distance is appropriate for those sharing space at an event.
▶ The public distance does not hold a specific connection.

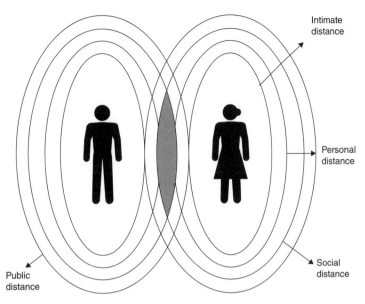

Social distances

When you are shy, you are often unable to maintain your boundaries; to keep yourself safely enveloped and secure. Your 'edges' are not clearly defined and people who are socially bold may crash into your personal space without permission. The personal space is generally reserved for those you trust so your defences are likely to be down and your ability to rally your forces and repel these intrusions may not be well developed, hence the feelings of being overwhelmed. It can look something like this:

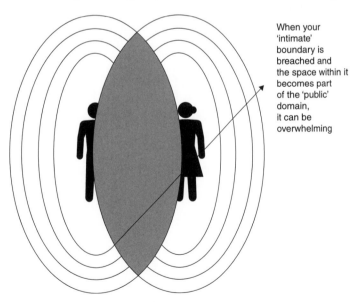

When your 'intimate' boundary is breached and the space within it becomes part of the 'public' domain, it can be overwhelming

When personal distance is breached

This depicts someone whose personal space has been invaded, and who is not very happy about it!

Ask yourself these questions:

What do you notice about the distance between you and the other person you're communicating with that feels natural for you?	
How do you feel when someone moves into your personal space uninvited?	

What strategies could you develop to strengthen your boundaries?

How do you 'read' someone else's signals about their tolerance to closeness?

To go back to Elizabeth's story, what she decided to try next time (in more favourable circumstances!) was to put the onus on the other person to shape the communication. She planned to do this by being curious, listening acutely to what they were saying and following their lead into the conversation by asking lots of follow-up questions. Listening is something we generally do really well when we're interested in something or likely to benefit from the information we gain so to 'evoke' a state of interest, or curiosity, is highly likely to be effective in building rapport. Although she had had an experience with her firm's client that was daunting, it was unusual for someone to be so hostile, she reasoned, so she decided to try again in a different setting – and it seemed to work!

In their book *Presence: Human Purpose and the Field of the Future*, Otto Scharmer et al. correlate the quality and depth of listening to transformational change. In their approach, they propose a listening model, the second stage of which is depicted below.

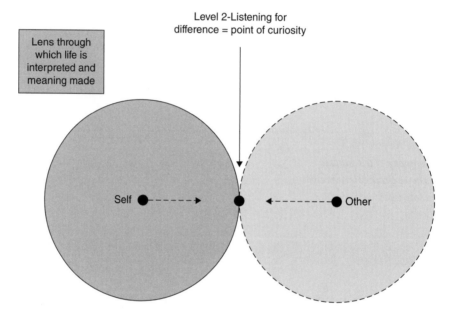

Second stage of the listening model

In this model, the left-hand circle labelled 'Self' in the middle, represents you in the centre of your own world. The dark grey area represents that world; it is the lens through which you make meaning. It comprises your thoughts, beliefs, values, prejudices, assumptions, convictions, experiences, cultural influences, learning and what you believe to be 'right' and 'wrong'. It is from the centre of your world that you make sense of your observations and experiences, and it is from these observations and experiences that you learn and make your choices. The world that you inhabit helps you to know yourself and people will know you (inasmuch as they can) from observing you act from this point.

Mostly we listen from this place; from the heart of our world-view. When someone says something that we already hold to be true, we hear it. When someone says something that does not already sit in our world, we don't 'hear' it.

Instead of being prisoners to our world-view, we can be open to other's world-views; we can be *curious*. We do this by moving (in our mind) from the centre, to the edge of our world. By leaving behind (or bracketing) our habitual patterns of thought, we can be open to others' views and ideas. Indeed, we can listen *for* difference.

What are the questions you naturally ask when you are curious?

- ▶ Who?
- ▶ When?
- ▶ What?
- ▶ Why?
- ▶ How?

They are 'tell me more' questions or 'open' questions.

The beauty of evoking a curious mindset is that you don't have to worry about the active listening techniques that we are encouraged to adopt, they flow naturally from genuine curiousness. You will find that you are: keeping eye contact, nodding, checking your understanding, making encouraging remarks and asking more clarifying questions – all signs of effective listening.

Activity 8.4

Listening to overcome your shyness

Next time you have a conversation, decide to have a 'curious mindset'.

See what happens when you get curious, genuinely. (This is different from feeling you *have* to ask someone a question, as Elizabeth was at her client dinner.)

Notice what happens to you when you don't agree with what someone is saying to you. What happens physically, physiologically or psychologically?

How do you feel if they hold a completely different set of values to you?

Curious listening check list	
Notice your body, what is it doing?	
Notice your mind, what is it doing?	
Notice your energy, what is it doing?	
Notice your reactions, what are they doing?	
How do you feel?	
What is your mood like?	

You may notice that it is quite possible to hear someone else's thoughts, ideas and opinions without losing your own. This is a strange statement, perhaps, but usually, we fight shy of those who don't think like us (or we fight with those who don't think like us to try to persuade them that they're wrong). These activities render us poor listeners.

By being curious, we are being open and receptive to new ways of thinking and doing things. This enables us to make changes that we otherwise might not make; hence, the correlation between listening and change.

Staying with behavioural shyness, here's another story that illustrates the terrain.

→ Anne's story – Going away to boarding school

'I was born into an Army family so, by the time I was 11, my schooling had been disrupted many times. For this reason, I was sent away to boarding school. My sisters were much older than me so they had been attending boarding school for some years beforehand and, being the youngest and, effectively, an only child, I had got used to being indulged and protected. Anyway, as it turned out, we went to different schools so I felt very much alone. I'll never forget sitting on the side of my allotted bed, watching my parents drive away. I had no idea how I was going to survive.

I had left my friends from home behind and I didn't know anyone at my new school. I felt extremely conspicuous and shy yet I knew that if I didn't reach out and make friends, I would be isolated and have a miserable time. So I decided to put on a façade and 'pretend' I was confident and happy. However, inside, I felt mortified.

I was very tall for my age, at least four inches taller than the next person in my class, so I adopted the habit of putting my weight on one leg so that I could lower my other hip and reduce my height. Added to the fact that I'd also developed a stoop, this made me look very timid.

I would observe others very closely to see if they could provide me with some behavioural clues that I could adopt to make me feel more confident, but it was never 'me', it was always an act. In the end, I just became a collage of other people and I began to lose the sense of who I was. If there were ever an occasion when I didn't have a 'mask', I would suffer all sorts of shyness symptoms. Blushing, sweating… but the worst was, I just couldn't hear. People would be talking to me and I couldn't process what they were saying. That was horrible. It was like my brain was trying to decipher a different language!'

Activity 8.5

 What would you do if you were in Anne's shoes?

What (if any) flaws do you think Anne's strategy had?	
What are the likely consequences of 'becoming a collage of other people'?	
Which of Anne's strategies have you used in the past and what was the outcome?	
What would you do if you were in Anne's position?	

Anne's story presents some of the same symptoms as Elizabeth's (see page 128) and also connects with Rose's story (see page 110) when she said she had ringing in her ears after making a presentation.

Although these stories come from three women, these kinds of reaction are not confined to the female gender.

This story comes from a man well into his retirement.

→ Herbert's story – A lifelong ambition

'I decided to learn the harp, it was a childhood ambition. I'd always wanted to play the harp, I don't know why, but the first record I bought was a harp solo.

I didn't start to learn until after I retired. I went to stay with some friends and the host was a harp player. In the course of conversation, I said to him, 'Would you like to gratify a childhood ambition?' He said yes, and then let me play. He taught me a few things and within half an hour, I was playing a simple tune. Then I decided to have lessons and eventually, I bought a harp of my own.

In a fit of boldness, I rang the local community orchestra and offered myself as a (beginner) harpist. They welcomed me and, because the music was so complex, one or two people wrote some simple parts for me. I became fairly fluent on certain pieces and was looking forward to our first concert – but it was dreadful. I just couldn't play. I felt tense and shy and my fingers seemed to move independently of my will. I think it was because I was fearful of doing a bad performance and that people would ridicule me. I was ridiculed a lot at school and I suppose I was trying to avoid repeating this when performing in the orchestra.'

Herbert speculated that his shyness might have been something to do with his upbringing.

'As a child, I was expected to be a charming extravert and, if I was too quiet, I was insulted by my mother. On the other hand, if I was too energetic or 'out there', she would make some icy comments or sarcastic put-downs. (I think this was the influence of the Victorian era. In those days, it was the view that children should be seen and not heard – but be socially adequate and make your parents proud! This double bind was impossible to resolve.) However, these comments made me feel 'small' and upset – and, if they were being made at a party, which they sometimes were, I felt conspicuous and embarrassed. I link these experiences to feeling shy in the orchestra – and to my reluctance to initiate conversations with people I don't know. I think it has affected me my whole life, although I don't think I'm shy now – at 93!'

Herbert helped his performance anxiety, to a large extent, by following the Alexander technique. This approach educated his body to find a balanced skeletal and muscular position that would give rise to full, and stress-free, function when he performed.

In this chapter, you have been presented with much material to help you overcome your shy behaviours. Practice makes perfect so take these ideas and experiment with making them your own.

Where to next?

This chapter has focused on the behavioural form of shyness and has outlined a number of ideas that may help combat feelings of ineptitude when engaged in a social interaction.

The next chapter will focus on the emotional form of shyness that manifests in the physiology. Typically, this shows up as the 'fight' or 'flight' response. When prepared for either of these options, the body is alert and infused with the chemicals that fuel 'staying in' (aggressively) or 'getting out' (quickly).

When the body is prepared for 'fight' or 'flight', it becomes super-charged with adrenaline which increases the heart and breathing rates. Blood vessels dilate, allowing more oxygen-rich blood to feed the muscles. The digestive process shuts down and an inclination to evacuate occurs. As we no longer live in a world where fight or flight is the most appropriate option, all these responses are happening as we stand still, trying to rally our resources. It's no wonder that we blush, sweat and stammer. The energy has to leak somewhere!

Keeping a note:	
What insights have you had as a result of reading this chapter?	

What are you going to do differently as a result of your insights?

How to deal with emotional shyness

> 'But when I knew her first she was so shy, as shy as a fawn, she really was. When people leaned to speak to her she would fold away from them, so that though she was still standing within their reach she was no longer accessible to them. She folded herself from them, they were no longer able to speak or go through with their touch. I put it down to her upbringing, a parson's daughter, and indeed, there was a good deal of Brontë about her.'
>
> Anna, speaking to Deeley about Kate in *Old Times*, by Harold Pinter.

Emotional shyness, described so eloquently above, creeps up on you and dominates social situations with feelings of self-consciousness and awkwardness. It is in these settings that the physiological symptoms of shyness manifest and, the more aware of them you are, the worse they get. These include such reactions as sweating, blushing, shaking, drying up, stomach cramps… and so on. If you're familiar with this type of shyness, you know what it's like and you understand how it prevents you from projecting yourself in an uninhibited way.

Knowing that you are likely to respond emotionally, you may experience what is called 'anticipatory anxiety', a condition that in itself evokes the kind of shyness reaction that you fear. In his book *Man's Search for Meaning*, Viktor Frankyl writes:

> 'An individual who is afraid of blushing when he enters a large room and faces many people will actually be more prone to blush under these circumstances.' (2004: 125)

Ironically, the opposite is also true inasmuch as:

> '... a "forced intention" makes impossible what one forcibly wishes.' (2004: 125)

So, being over anxious, and worrying obsessively about your prospective social encounters, can exacerbate the shyness response. Also, being over-intentional about not having it, makes it more likely to happen.

In this chapter, you are introduced to people who suffer from this condition. They share their experiences and the methodologies they've developed for overcoming this overarching form of shyness.

In this way, you will learn how to:

▶ Understand more about what happens in situations charged with emotional shyness

▶ Identify strategies that enable you to put yourself into settings that usually trigger a shy response

▶ Manage your physiological response to emotional shyness

→ Kate's story – Being among groups of strangers

'I hate any social situation, like networking or attending a party, where you don't know the people you're going to meet – and perhaps, you don't want to! Being amongst a big group of people like this makes me realize how shy I am.

I don't like work groups either, where you get together with colleagues. There always seem to be one or two people in them who are lobbying to be heard; wanting to be liked or just being 'clubby'. I guess they're vying for professional position. I don't like the politics of that.

On these occasions, I 'forget' how to interact. I stop talking. Lose everything. My confidence. My social skills. And don't see it as a challenge but as something that is petrifying – and I'm not a petrified person really.

I ask myself why anyone would be interested in listening and talking to me once I had said hello – actually, I don't know *how* to say hello, so I don't even do that! I prefer to avoid these situations altogether. The groups I particularly don't like are around 20+ in number.

The common theme is I don't like people I don't know and, when I'm faced with them, I'm overcome with shyness. I think the underlying anxiety is 'Will people like me?' And if they don't… there's no logic in this. It makes no sense because there are no consequences if people don't like me.

I think the first time I became shy was as a child. I was a 'cute kid' so, if there was an occasion when someone had to be thanked for giving a speech or something, I was always chosen to go up and present the flowers. I hated it and became quite shy about it. Really self-conscious. I didn't want to be put in the limelight and I certainly didn't want the other kids to think I was the favourite because then I'd get teased.

My most recent challenge was a friend's 50th birthday. Everyone was there in pairs and I felt self-conscious because I wasn't in a pair myself. I experienced a progressive sense of becoming shyer and shyer. I could feel my confidence just draining away, so much so that I eventually lost the art of conversation and had to leave!'

Kate's story is not unusual, yet we can see how difficult it makes life for her – and for the rest of us who suffer in these 'unstructured' situations where we try to hold our own among those we don't know. The amount of time and energy we consume anticipating, and then attending these events, is often out of all proportion to the value they deliver. Yet, they continue to dog our social and professional calendars. Surely there must be a way of removing this onerous obstacle, known as shyness, from our consciousness?

So, what would you do if you were Kate, anticipating the 50th birthday party of her friend?

Activity 9.1

Planning a strategy

See whether you can plan out a strategy below:

Before	
During	
After	

Talking further, Kate said that there is something about the social aspects of shyness that she finds more overwhelming than professional situations. In her work, she stands up in front of big audiences and gives motivating talks. She also manages to be confident among groups of colleagues with whom she collaborates for work. 'In fact', Kate says, 'if you were to ask these people 'Is Kate shy?', they would say 'Absolutely not!' They would never associate that characteristic with me, yet I get really shaky and shy a lot of the time!'

However, below is what Kate does to overcome her shyness in social situations. See whether she has any ideas that you can adopt to help you out in similar situations.

Before	
	I speak to the hostess beforehand to see if there's going to be anyone there with mutual friends or interests. (Last time I attended a party, the hostess was a good friend and she told me it would be fine. She knew I was coming by myself so she reassured me that she would introduce me to some nice people.)
	I give myself a good talking to and ensure that I feel good in my appearance.
	I make sure I have my transportation organized and my 'escape strategy' in place – which I may not use! (This would be something like: the number of a cab company in my bag, enough cash to pay for a taxi, my car parked in an accessible position, a friend to collect me... and so on.)
	I give myself a task such as having to introduce myself to the people closest to me. Or, I must speak to at least four people. Or, I must find someone with whom I share an interest or acquaintances.
	I prepare a few things to say about myself – and some introductory phrases to help me enter a conversation.
During	
	I familiarize myself with the layout of the party so that I can move around if I feel conspicuous standing still. Where are the toilets, drink, food and so on.
	I find a group where someone's looking up and I can catch their eye.
	I hold myself to a time limit. You have to do it for this amount of time and then you can go. You arrive at 8.00 and come away by 10.
	I look for people who are shyer than me in the room. (Last time, I ended up talking to the MP. He puts on a public façade because he's shyer than me and I found myself looking after him. This made me feel less shy!)
	I return to my host or hostess to see if they'll introduce me to someone else – or give me a job.

After	
	Reward myself for completing the challenges that I set myself.
	Contact the host to say 'Thank you!'
	Follow-up on any contacts I made that I'd like to keep.
	Think about what worked and what didn't work.
	Accept another invitation to a party.

Activity 9.2

Networking and new contacts

Do some networking and make two new contacts.

Identify an event to go to. It might be a conference, a seminar or an event designed for networking – and plan to make two new contacts. (These are people that you will follow up with.)

Here's a useful process:

▶ Go through the list of attendees and mark out a couple that you'd like to meet.

▶ Find out a little bit about them. You can start on LinkedIn or on some other networking site – you may even find a photograph.

▶ Ask members of your current network if they know them and could introduce you.

▶ Contact them in advance to say that you'll be there and that you hope to meet them or seek them out at the event. (There may be a list of attendees for particular talks or workshops. You can then approach people one by one to see whether they can point you in the right direction or introduce you.)

OR go in 'cold':

▶ Put yourself down for a talk or workshop.

▶ Strike up a conversation with the person sitting next to you.

▶ Aim to return home with two new business cards and a promise of a follow-up meeting.

Here is an inspiring story of a young woman who suffers from shyness yet succeeds in an area that you would think would be the last place a shy person would succeed!

Vanessa is a young girl of 14. She has a passion for singing yet she feels really shy about doing it. When she stands in front of the microphone, she gets really nervous. 'I go bright red immediately. I can't stop it. And I always think "Oh God what am I doing? I'm bright red and I'm standing in front of a whole load of people and they're all looking at me waiting for me to sing to them!"

→ Vanessa's story – A passion for singing

'I love singing. I'm singing all the time at home so I decided to attend summer camp with a friend. It's called: Pop Star to Super Star. It began with an audition. I was really nervous. I felt bright red and hot when I had to stand up and sing in front of the judges, but I pushed through the redness and the hotness because I knew that I enjoyed singing, and when I'm enjoying it, my singing is much better, which is why I was there.

When I started singing classes in the first place, I was really uncomfortable with it. But I did it with a friend and we messed around together. That put me at my ease. To start with we sang a duet in a show. That was really fun. My friend and I rehearsed it to perfection. We worked on it for five months and created the choreography too. We really enjoyed doing it and, because we were together, it didn't feel too bad.

I think I've always been shy. I'm always shy when I'm starting something new. Performing in public makes me shy. I can perform in front of just one person, or perhaps a group of friends, but in public, that's different. I think it's the fact that everyone's watching me, everyone is paying me attention. I'm always scared that they'll laugh at me or think that what I'm doing is no good.

The worst thing is when my friend says I'm going bright red and then it gets worse and worse and I just want to hide in a corner until I'm a normal colour again!

Also, I've been laughed at by boys at school so that might be in the back of my mind too. Most of the time they don't mean any harm but still, it does affect me!'

Activity 9.3

 What would you do in Vanessa's situation?

Before	
During	
After	

Vanessa shows huge courage and resilience in the face of her shy responses. She says: 'I've been taught to take my courage in my two hands and tell myself to do the best I can.'

This is how Vanessa manages her shyness around singing. Again, look for ideas that you may be able to use yourself.

Before	Rehearse. Rehearse. Rehearse. I learn the song really well and once I've got it nailed, I let go of the stress and try to enjoy it.
	Persistence – and good support. I practise on my own and in front of people I trust.
	I attend singing lessons so I've taken a lot of feedback and done a lot of learning around how to sing properly. This has built my confidence.
During	Just do it! I was really nervous and my knees were shaking but I just sang through it and no one noticed.
	When I start singing, I sort of lose myself to the song and, knowing I've got the support behind me in the form of the music, I know I'm not alone.
	Put everything into the performance and keep going to the end. Let go of any mistakes.
After	If there is some learning for the next time, I'll take it away and work on it.
	I feel really proud and really happy when I've done it.
	When I walked off the stage at the end of my performance, it felt amazing and I wished I could go back out there and do it all again!

After Vanessa shared her story, she said:

'It's because I just love doing it that I overcome my shyness. I love it more than my shyness.'

This is such a profound statement. If shyness takes you to the point of paralysis, it is worth thinking about what it is that you're doing, why you're doing it and the importance you place upon it. This is a way of diminishing self-consciousness and raising other-consciousness. Even if it's only for the duration of your activity, other-consciousness, whether it is focus on an activity or another person, will enable your inhibitions to be superseded.

Look beyond yourself to overcome your shyness!

Activity 9.4

 Visualization

Your task	What was your experience?
Find a space and relax. *This is an opportunity to go for gold. No one will see you or comment on your practice so find a quiet, private space, close your eyes, breathe deeply and relax.*	
Envisage yourself as you would like to be in a social situation that usually brings you anxiety. Describe your attributes and capabilities. What do you look like? What are you doing?	

Create a specific, detailed image.

Build a technicolour scenario with you in the centre of it feeling great and doing a wonderful job. Where are you? What are you doing? When is this happening?

See yourself from above.

Take a view of yourself as if you were watching someone else. This helps you experience the context and see yourself objectively.

Put your experience in your body.

Feel what's happening to your body; the touch, smell, sensation of doing the thing that you're visualizing.

Believe it!

When you have finished the exercise, do it again – in more detail!

Visualization is a great way of clarifying the way forward, especially when it is alternated with practice. Although you can't become an expert on visualization alone, it is a surprisingly powerful technique that enables you to 'rehearse' your dreams and bring them to reality. The 'bringing them to reality' bit is based upon the fact that when you envisage something, exactly the same neural pathways are used – and grooved – as if you were living your dream in practice. So, the more you do it, the easier it will be to manifest it.

Andrew is a young man who is mid-way through his university course. Although shy, he has worked out some ways to help him make social headway in this challenging environment.

→ Andrew's story – Making headway at university

'I don't know why I'm shy. I think it's because I'm quite self-conscious. When people get to know me I'm quite talkative but at the outset, I'm concerned about what they think of me and that inhibits me. I've been shy for quite a while. It's part of my personality. It's part of being in my family.

When I meet new people, I seize up and don't know what to say. I get nervous because I don't want to make a fool of myself and I don't want to say anything too provocative or rude. I wouldn't be able to banter or joke with new people in case they thought I was being serious and I was drawn into an argument. I'm very conscious about what I say, I don't swear or anything so that they don't have any reason to hate me. But if they don't hate me, it's because I haven't said anything interesting enough! I can't win!

I'm a lot better since going to university. Mainly because I have to be! If you are too shy at the beginning of university, you get mucked up for the next three years. You need to make friends in the first year otherwise it's hard to survive the rest of the course.

To make some friends at the beginning of my course, I decided to join a sports club because I knew that doing sport was a good way of meeting people.

I do go to some parties. I tend to go with the same group of people and I know I'll encounter other people I know so it is quite comfortable now. However, if I'm standing on my own, I move about a bit to see if I can bump into people I know. If this doesn't work, when it gets to midnight, I just leave.

I wouldn't approach anyone in a club, especially girls. I just turn to stone. I'm pretty sure I'm invisible! I'm hoping I'll get better at coping with my shyness.

I'm going to spend my third year at university in France. This might help.

The best piece of advice I was given was 'Don't care what they think about you. If they like you, you'll see them again. If they don't, that's OK, you'll never have to see them again.'

Andrew found some great ways of creating the bridge between his shyness and his desire to make the best of his university experience. Some of these approaches may suggest strategies to you.

Andrew's story is interesting because it is full of the dichotomous struggles that are so characteristic of shy people. For instance: 'I don't swear or anything so that they don't have any reason to hate me. But if they don't hate me, it's because I haven't said anything interesting enough!' and 'I just turn to stone. I'm pretty sure I'm invisible!' The courage that he shows in taking off to France for his final year is legion so, although he may see his shyness as a 'weakness', it pulls super-human strength from him.

In all these stories, there are similar themes. The overwhelming notion that you're conspicuous, being judged and being found wanting. The physiological response to these thoughts often overrides your ability to think properly because you are being prepared for 'fight' or 'flight', which is about action, not thought!

We've already seen that, once triggered, all the internal responses to 'fight' or 'flight' happen at once: a release of adrenaline; increased heart rate; rapid breathing; energy to the muscles; a desire to empty the bowels! While, all the time, you're trying to access your mind and look poised and present!

Activity 9.5

A room full of strangers

When you are in a room full of strangers, relax!

Most of us encounter times when we are compelled to enter social situations knowing few, or no, people. This is not an appealing prospect by any measure! However, there are several ways of making this more tolerable, even intriguing. It is said that we are about six handshakes away from anyone in the world. The chances are, therefore, that you will encounter someone who knows someone you do when you are in a room full of strangers. Here's the challenge: when you go into a room where you don't think you know anyone, find someone to talk to and see whether you can find the connection that links you in the first three minutes of your conversation. This connection may be a person but it may also be a shared interest, a university, professional expertise, a cultural experience, a passion or an intention. Write down your triumphs!

| Networking event: |
| Date: |

| Who I spoke to: | |
| The points of connection between us: | |

→ Some thoughts to take away

Deep breathing: This is a great way to slow everything down and to stem the flood of rising shyness, especially when you are alarmed or overwhelmed. It involves breathing into the abdomen; its rise and fall being indicative of the correctness of your breathing. Here's how to do it:

1 Stand in a relaxed way (or lie down if this is possible). Scan your body for areas of tension and try to soften the muscles as you pass your attention over them.

2 Put your hands on your abdomen. (This is to give you a feedback mechanism so you know when you are breathing correctly.)

3 Take a deep breath until your hands are rising on your abdomen.

4 Using your abdominal muscles, push the air back out again. (Although your chest will rise and fall too, it is the abdomen that should lead. This ensures that you are using your diaphragm correctly.)

5 Continue breathing in this way slowly: three seconds in, six seconds out. Build a steady rhythm that sees your abdomen moving like a wave-form. (If you're lying down, you may fall asleep!)

Focus on other people or the importance of your activity – if you are more interested in the other people you encounter or the activity you are engaged with, you are much more likely to escape the symptoms of shyness. Remember Vanessa saying: 'It's because I just love doing it (singing) that I overcome my shyness. I love it more than my shyness.'

Put your situation into a larger context – think about why you are in the situation and what it will lead to. Focus on tomorrow and how you will feel when your ordeal is over. By bringing this to mind during attacks of shyness, you can loosen the grip of emotional shyness and find instant relief.

Remember a time when you excelled and flood yourself with those feelings. Similar to the way Pavlov conditioned his dogs to salivate when they heard a bell, you can condition yourself to experience inner confidence when cued by an external trigger. This is how you do it:

1 Consider a time when you felt superbly confident.

2 Envisage it fully and colourfully and re-evoke the inner state you enjoyed at that time.

3 Anchor or create a cue for this state by forming an external trigger. (While you're in the fullness of the state you recalled, pinch your thumb and forefinger together, for instance.)

4 Next time you want to feel that same inner state, pinch your thumb and forefinger together to trigger the cue and you will be filled with your desired state again.

Smile – when you smile, your facial colour naturally reddens. It distracts people from seeing your blushing as embarrassment and encourages them to see it as friendly.

Smile!

A cautionary note: Try to avoid using your drug of choice to escape the symptoms of shyness!

Where to next?

Having looked at three of the four domains of shyness, we are now going to close the loop by entering the mind. This strand of shyness is woven through, and compounds, the messages that are picked up through the other three forms of shyness. No doubt you will see some of the resonances in the stories you have already read.

In the next chapter you will learn about:

▶ The vicious cycle that keeps you in the thrall of your shyness
▶ The Ladder of Inference – a thinking process that allows you to challenge and re-wire your mental circuitry

The importance of staying present – not rooted in the past or speculating about the future.

Keeping a note:	
What insights have you had as a result of reading this chapter?	

What are you going to
do differently as a result
of your insights?

How to deal with 'rational' shyness

We have travelled across a lot of the territory of shyness; circumstantial, behavioural and, in the previous chapter, emotional. Now, we're going to move into that tricky area of the mind.

In this chapter, you will learn about:

▶ The vicious cycle that keeps you in the thrall of your shyness

▶ The Ladder of Inference – a thinking process that allows you to challenge and re-wire your mental circuitry

▶ The importance of staying present – not rooted in the past or speculating about the future

Rational (or irrational) shyness is based upon cognitions of the mind. These cognitions may be rational and reasonable analyses of past situations. For instance: if you were bullied at school, it would stand to reason that you wouldn't put yourself in the way of the bullies. These cognitions may also be irrational and unreasonable such as habitual negative anticipatory messages that dominate the mind and undermine any chance of confidence. Whether these are rooted in the past or imagined from the future, these thought patterns take you away from the present circumstances and steal your resources.

These habitual thinking patterns may look something like this: (Starting from top, left)

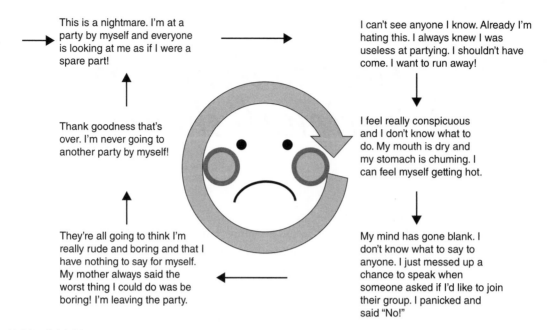

This is a nightmare. I'm at a party by myself and everyone is looking at me as if I were a spare part!

I can't see anyone I know. Already I'm hating this. I always knew I was useless at partying. I shouldn't have come. I want to run away!

Thank goodness that's over. I'm never going to another party by myself!

I feel really conspicuous and I don't know what to do. My mouth is dry and my stomach is chuming. I can feel myself getting hot.

They're all going to think I'm really rude and boring and that I have nothing to say for myself. My mother always said the worst thing I could do was be boring! I'm leaving the party.

My mind has gone blank. I don't know what to say to anyone. I just messed up a chance to speak when someone asked if I'd like to join their group. I panicked and said "No!"

Habitual thinking patterns

As you can probably see, the rational form of shyness is integrated with the other three forms. When active, it compounds and exacerbates the impact of the circumstantial, emotional and behavioural domains of shyness. And it is particularly tricky because it 'seduces' you to think and believe things that are not founded on truth, but appear to be true because there is logic in there somewhere, albeit twisted or disconnected. The other feature of this form of shyness is its habitual and unquestioned repetition. Onlookers are quite able to detect it and may say 'Here we go again!' to the protestations of the harbinger. However, let's see if we can pluck it out and replace it with a more positive reasoning.

What expectations do you have before you go into a social situation?

'I'm going to hate it!'

'I'm going to make a complete fool of myself!'

How can you reframe these thoughts so that they don't hang over you and invite self-fulfilment? (Reframing was a technique introduced in Chapter 1.)

'I'm going to make the best of it!'

'I'm going to do myself proud!'

Let's illustrate this more graphically using someone's real-life experience.

Maisie is a young woman who is at the senior end of her schooling. She is intelligent and a hard worker. Her story is an illustration of how undermining the mind can be. The complex logic and its effect can be seen clearly. See which bits speak to you.

→ Maisie's story – A competitive speech

'Making speeches is something that I don't like. I had to do one at school. It was really scary. It was a prize giving and all the Governors were there. I was terrified.

The Headmaster and Deputy Heads were sitting behind me and, as I went to the podium, I felt as if I was going to trip over and die. I walked on and off really slowly. Half way through, I thought my skirt was over my bum. I felt really conspicuous and embarrassed. I couldn't get the idea out of my head.

My Headmaster introduced me and then tapped me on my shoulder when I was about to go on. I nearly collapsed. It was supposed to be supportive but I felt that my knees were going to give way and that I would fall over. I could see all the pupils looking at me, my mother, my father, my friends. I don't think this helped. I died inside. When I was reading the speech, I knew I had to look up from time to time but I didn't want to. I had to force myself to do so because I didn't want to be one of those people who just look down to read so I just had to do it. Then I lost my place and lost my flow. It was dreadful. I have no idea how it went. I went into a haze of black.

I only survived because of the pressure. I had to do it. I couldn't say 'No!' because I wrote the speech in the first place. It was a competition but because there was no one in the category above me, I had to represent the higher age group. The speech was all about my experience at the school. I'd written this hilarious speech, which I liked, but it didn't fit the culture of the school so the Deputy Head changed it. It wasn't mine therefore. It was his. It had to fit the mould of the school so it ended up being his speech.'

You can see that Maisie's mind was playing all sorts of undermining tricks on her. She evoked a series of horrors. First, that she hated giving speeches (past); second, that her skirt was over her bum (present); and third, that she would trip up (future). All of these negative fantasies – past, present and future – undermined her confidence and distracted her attention. However, as you will see in the next excerpt, Maisie used her mind to create a more positive aspect and she left with a sense of pride having pushed through the challenge and learned a lot from it.

As you read the remainder of the story, look out for those things that Maisie did that suggest ideas to you and note them down in the table below:

Activity 10.1

 How could you make this a positive experience if you were Maisie?

Before	

During	✍

After	✍

Here's the rest of her story:

'I overcame this because of the pressure, and I felt I had no *real* choice. So, I practised 50 million times and told myself, 'Of course you can do it!' I knew I wasn't a turd, actually, and the only thing I had to worry about was not falling over. I didn't want to let myself down with everyone watching me. Then, by the time I got up there, I knew I couldn't back out because if I did, I would be humiliated. So, I either had to get on with it and overcome my fears of doing a speech I wasn't fully comfortable with, or back out – but then I would be humiliated and everyone in the school would witness my failure.

I also had lots of encouragement from people: parents, friends, teachers, the Headmaster, so I focused on that. I thought: 'If they think I can do it, then I must be able to.' I'd also rehearsed in front of the Headmaster and his deputies and they were happy with it. And, as they were the ones I had to impress, I took it as personal encouragement.

I didn't really volunteer, when the Deputy Head asked me, I thought, 'Well, this is a bit of a challenge but if I did it, it would impress the Headmaster and help me become a Prefect.' By showing my enthusiasm and commitment to the school, I would differentiate myself. Otherwise, I'm just another pupil. So I looked for all the positives. Even though all this added to the pressure, I found ways of finding the positives so that I fed my belief that I could do it. I focused on the outcome because I felt that that would pull me through. By the time I got up, I knew I couldn't turn around so I just got on with it.

Although I thought it was a little boring and I could have done better, I was also proud of myself. Now I wouldn't mind doing it again. In fact, although I'd still be nervous, I'd be happy to do it again.'

Activity 10.2

Maisie's tactics

What did you notice about Maisie's tactics? Which ones do you think you could adopt and how?

Maisie's tactics	How could you make use of this tactic?
She used the pressure to compel her to do something she'd rather not do.	
She rehearsed 50 million times.	
She gave herself positive self-talk.	
She adopted the philosophy 'fake it 'til you make it!'	
She didn't want to let herself down so she put as much into it as possible.	

Once she had started, she couldn't stop (or she'd be publicly humiliated).	
She found lots of encouragement from her close circle.	
She looked for the positives.	
She used it to distinguish herself as a prospective prefect. She likes a challenge!	
She focused on the outcome and was able to diminish the enormousness (in her mind) of the speech.	
Laugh at yourself before someone else does!	

By the way, Maisie became a prefect!

Let's look at the mental process we go through to make a decision or take an action. Chris Argyris, Professor Emeritus at Harvard Business School and known for developing the notion of the 'Learning Organization', proposes *The Ladder of Inference* as a way of understanding, and being able to challenge, habitual thought processes that lead us to making decisions or taking action, sometimes unquestioned and ineffective decisions and actions. This is what it looks like:

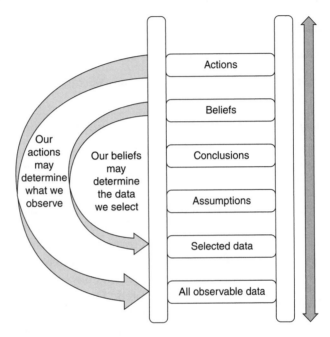

The Ladder of Inference

The above illustration maps the process from making an observation to taking an action or making a decision.

▶ Starting from the bottom rung, we have a wide set of data available to us.

▶ Moving up the ladder, we select or notice specific data based on our prior experience.

▶ Continuing up, we make some (unquestioned) assumptions about the data we have selected to notice. This is where you add meaning to the data you have selected to observe.

▶ Then we draw conclusions about it based upon the assumptions we have made and the 'facts' we have interpreted.

▶ We use these conclusions to develop a set of beliefs and expectations.

▶ We take action or make a decision based upon our beliefs. It feels 'right' to us.

This all happens at lightning speed and out of consciousness. However, by attending to this process, we can identify disconnects in our logic and pluck out 'bad' thinking habits that render us shy.

Let's look at the ladder from Maisie's point of view:

The Ladder of Inference	Maisie's beliefs
Observable data	I'm looking out over a room full of people.
Selected data	I can see all the pupils staring blankly at me.
Assumptions	They're staring at me blankly because they're bored and think I'm doing a rubbish job.
Conclusions	They're right. I'm not doing a good job of making this presentation. It's boring.
Beliefs	I'm not very good at giving presentations.
Actions	I'm going to avoid giving presentations in the future.

This approach helps us to understand why we go into recursive loops. For instance, you begin to select data based upon your beliefs. You believe that you're not very good at giving presentations so you look for the evidence that proves this to be true. (In Maisie's case: I'm not very good at giving presentations because, when I do, people stare blankly at me and are bored.) Or, you take an action/inaction that creates a situation (in which there is observable data for you to select from) so that you can verify the correctness of this action/inaction. (Again, in Maisie's case: I'm not going to give a presentation because I don't want to bore a room full of people.)

So, what do you do about this?

 Activity 10.3

Checking your assumptions

Think of a situation where you use 'rational' argument to undermine your social confidence (e.g. giving a presentation or going to a networking event).

Ask yourself (or ask a trusted friend or colleague to ask you):

What actions am I taking that are unhelpful to me? (Or, What behaviours am I adopting that are unhelpful to me?)	
What belief do I hold that results in these actions/ behaviours?	
What are the conclusions that I have drawn that underpin this belief?	
What assumptions am I making that support my conclusion?	
What data am I basing my assumptions upon? Are these assumptions correct?	

What other assumptions or conclusions could I draw from the data?	
If I selected other data, what different assumptions or conclusions could I draw from them?	
Are there any stages in the process I tend to skip? If so, why? What am I avoiding?	
How am I going to use **The Ladder of Inference** to challenge my habitual thinking process?	
Who can I ask to take me through my meaning-making sequence? (It's sometimes easier to be answerable to another who does not collude with your habits and leaps of abstraction!)	

Here's another story from someone whose 'head' gets in the way of his ability to perform.

→ Robert's story – That shrinking feeling!

'I was co-facilitating a workshop for a top team in which my role was not particularly clear and it felt trivial from the outset. I was stepping into someone else's shoes so did not have much ownership of the material. What's more, the timing was tight, so there were some good reasons why it was best for me not to speak too much. But the more the workshop continued without my speaking, the more self-conscious I became about not adding any value and that became a very uncomfortable situation.

I'm often quite nervous and self-conscious, but it's something I can overcome when I'm clear about what my role is and when I have accepted personal responsibility for making something happen. But this feeling of being a 'bit part' was very unsatisfactory and silencing. I don't feel I was shy, per se, but I was extremely self-conscious – and internally very critical – so I wasn't able to focus on the participants. Naturally this gets in the way when you're facilitating a workshop!

The internal conversation in my head was louder than the external conversation and went something like: 'Don't say anything stupid!' 'Only say something if you've got something valuable to say.' 'But how do you know that you have something valuable to say!' A bit of a double-edged sword, really. My attention became internal and a critical preoccupation found fault with, trivialised and ridiculed what I wanted to say, and the longer I didn't speak up the more that internal voice had a hold.

I get this shrinking feeling when I'm not adding value, and that's what happened. I just wanted to disappear and run away from the whole situation. I felt completely irrelevant. It was a really unrewarding situation to be in.

I have messages in my head from my childhood. Things like 'Who do you think you are?' 'What do you know?!' I know they're not relevant now but they get very loud when my confidence disappears.'

In terms of *The Ladder of Inference*, Robert said that if he doesn't speak up when he feels himself slipping away, it becomes harder and harder to do so until it feels impossible. In other words, the longer he withholds his intervention (action), the stronger is his conviction that he has nothing valuable to say (assumption and belief).

Let's look a little closer at the 'rational' domain of shyness and we'll do so through the eyes of Dr Steven Peters, a psychiatrist specializing in how the human mind can enable us to be happy, confident and successful. Apart from authoring a very successful book entitled *The Chimp Paradox*, Dr Peters was credited for helping Sir Chris Hoy and Victoria Pendleton win their gold medals for cycling at the 2012 Olympic games. He did this by helping them master their 'inner chimp'.

Dr Peters proposes that if we are not being happy, confident and successful, it is because our minds are not being managed properly. Further, he points towards three aspects of our minds that are battling for control of our thoughts, feelings and actions, one of which, the 'inner chimp', is generally out of control and running roughshod over our lives.

This is how it works. We live in our frontal lobe. This is where our logical thinking takes place. The 'inner chimp' lives in the limbic. This is where our feelings, impressions and emotions are located – and where we indulge our tendency to catastrophize. The parietal is where the computer sits. It runs the whole system and is in service to the other components of the brain. However, he calculates, for about 90 per cent of the time the 'inner chimp' is in control, wielding its considerable power. 'The chimp' is instinctive, indulgent and irrational and, while seeking to satisfy our inner drives, it highjacks our mind. Unmanaged, it acts before we have a chance to think so we become coloured by this 'chimpish' aspect of ourselves. To counter its dominance in our lives, Dr Peters advises talking to our 'inner chimp' and helping it to be calm and collected. This will enable us to bring it under new management; our management – rather than let it manage us. We can do this by:

▶ Letting it have its say for a few moments (in a safe environment) before you take command of it

▶ Using logic to spike its guns – sane reasoning, facts and logic

▶ Distracting it through techniques such as deep breathing, counting to ten and promising it a reward where it can express itself freely – in play or physical activity

Just think… If the power of your 'inner chimp' can prevent you from living your life in a happy, confident and successful way, just think what you can achieve by harnessing its power and managing it to your advantage!

→ Being present

When we are torturing ourselves with thoughts of what has happened to us in the past, or fears about what will happen to us in the future, we get dragged out of the present and less of our energy and attention is available to deal with what's on our agenda.

As we have seen in the stories above, being shy in the 'rational' domain is beset with spurious and unhelpful thoughts of past and future and, if we are dogged by our past or distracted by our future, we miss out on life as it is happening. Just think of those moments when you've missed what someone has been saying because you've been worrying about your next meeting.

Although we need the context of the past and the future to take informed actions and make decisions, we could benefit by taking control over the amount of time we spend dwelling in these virtual places. In this way, we could be fully present and wholehearted about what we're doing, now.

Patsy Rodenburg, voice coach to the acting profession and author of *The Second Circle: How to use positive energy for success in every situation*, coined the notion of three circles of energy, each one having its own distinctive qualities that condition us to engage successfully in life, or not.

Activity 10.4

Definitions

Have a look at the definitions below and think about how you are in your interactions and whether this frame has any value for you. (You can move rapidly between each circle and be in or out of each one in a physical, intellectual, emotional and spiritual way – and not necessarily all at the same time.)

First circle – This is the circle where your energy is constantly returning to yourself. You consume yourself energetically, so to speak, going inwards and withdrawing. When your energy goes 'in', it is not available to others. In fact, they may feel isolated, shut out, rejected. The flavour of this circle is 'the past'. It is gone, no longer available.

Third circle – This is the circle where your energy is sent out into the world in a generalized way. These people take up a lot of space. Their voices are loud. Their movements are exaggerated. The flavour of this circle is 'the future' – pushing out, controlling, dominating.

Second circle – This is the circle where your energy is focused on what is going on now. Whether you are engaged in a conversation with a person, reading a book or listening to music, it represents the 'give and take' of life as it happens. The flavour of this circle is 'the present', it is the circle of equality, of intimacy, of attention. It is where we are confident in our bodies and wholehearted about what we're doing; passionate and in our 'flow'. Listening with curiosity (Chapter 8) enables you to get into the second circle.

Patsy Rosenburg says: 'If you're not able to get present, you cannot succeed.' She adds that if we do something in fear, we are not present.

Put your observations in the grid below:

What do you notice about being in:	What do you plan to do differently?
First circle: (e.g. My mind wanders when I'm bored or distracted.)	First circle: (e.g. Develop self-awareness and discipline to bring my mind back.)
Second circle: (e.g. I'm really happy and productive and my relationships are reciprocal.)	Second circle: (e.g. Use curiosity to access the second circle more often.)

<table>
<tr>
<td>

Third circle:

(e.g. I'm off balance, working too hard to compensate for feeling awkward.)

</td>
<td>

Third circle:

(e.g. Reign in my energy and attend to others' needs.)

</td>
</tr>
</table>

This chapter has focused on the mind and how it's powerful pull can take you off balance and accentuate your shyness.

With attention and discipline, you can bring your mind under greater control, reverse the negative self-talk and replace it with a more positive narrative.

→ Social media and the four domains of shyness

A note about social media before leaving the fourth domain of shyness.

People are increasingly using social media to ameliorate their shyness. The reasons for this are that social media offers:

▶ The ability to avoid *circumstantial* shyness by obviating the need to be physically present in any situation

▶ The ability to avoid being seen as *emotionally* shy by being invisible to the other when the reactions are taking place

▶ The ability to avoid being seen as *behaviourally* inept because the behaviours are mediated through the internet and can appear more skilled virtually than they are in reality

▶ The ability to think *rationally* before responding to any message because the whole relationship is time shifted

Social media offers users the opportunity to strike up virtual conversations and to build relationships with people who may never be encountered in the flesh (although, not with online dating!) It offers a 'mask' that shy people can hide behind so that what feels impossible face-to-face becomes easy over the internet. Often quite intimate details are exchanged or contained on profiles so that knowledge of someone is built up rapidly – if they share the truth, that is! So there are many advantages for shy people to connect with others in this way. (Apparently, Facebook harbours more shy people than socially confident and outgoing people.)

Social media, therefore, is an avenue that allows:

▶ Conversations to be relevant and to the point – avoiding small talk

▶ Time to elapse while you consider your response

▶ Long-haul communications to be formed with ease

▶ Access to people who would not naturally be included in your network

▶ Invention of the person you want to be known as

▶ Observation over a period of time so you can choose when, how, if, you interact

▶ Control of your social boundaries

▶ Potential life friendships or partnerships

▶ Membership of special interest groups and related networks

Of course, there may come a time when you meet the person you've connected with online and, if you have projected a different persona to the one you have in reality, or built yourself up in a way that you find difficult to live up to, this could be a nerve-wracking (and disappointing) meeting. Your prior sharing, however, could have cleared a lot of the social groundwork so that you can move more swiftly into a deeper relationship, avoiding all those potentially embarrassing first steps. Whatever, enter this cyberspace with your eyes open and decide how you're going to use it for no record is every *really* lost or deleted. Ask yourself: if your social experimentation came back to haunt you, how would you feel?!

We have now come to the end of our journey through the four different domains of shyness. Hopefully, you will have discovered things about yourself that you didn't know before and have developed some ways of building greater social confidence. But how often have you thought you'd make some behavioural changes before and why did they not succeed? Breaking your old habits is not easy because they feel natural – even if they're not gratifying!

We know who we are when we do what we normally do!

Where to next?

So, how are you going to create a new sense of normality?

In the next chapter, we're going to advance towards helping you:

▶ Break old (unhelpful) habits

▶ Develop new (helpful) habits

▶ Embed the new habits in your behavioural catalogue so that you can confidently develop effective strategies for overcoming your shyness

Don't forget to reflect on your learning and capture the main points below.

Keeping a note:	
What insights have you had as a result of reading this chapter?	

What are you going to do differently as a result of your insights?

Adopting and maintaining new habits to overcome shyness

Having completed an exploration of the different forms of shyness, you should be in a position to know yourself better, to understand the habitual patterns that undermine you and to find some solutions that will enable you to build social confidence. But how do you form and maintain your new habits? In this chapter, we're going to start pulling it all together and help you plan ways to embed your strategies for overcoming shyness. Specifically, this chapter will cover:

▶ The nature of habit

▶ How to break, create and embed new habits

▶ How to use your self-knowledge to outwit your sabotaging tendencies

▶ How to establish long-lasting and life-changing social behaviours

Psychologically speaking, a habit is defined as an involuntary behavioural pathway between a stimulus (a thought or situation that acts as a trigger) and a response (an action or a behaviour). For example, we may respond to stress (whether it be mental, physical or emotional) by picking up a cigarette, having a drink or consuming one or two bars of chocolate.

Habits are not all bad. Indeed, some of our habits are life-sustaining, literally. Bodily functions like breathing, digesting food, pumping blood, regulating body temperature (all of which promote functional balance, or homeostasis) are controlled out of consciousness by the hypothalamus, the autonomic nervous system and the endocrine system. We would not want to be conscious of these multiple complex processes, not only because we may not have the capability to manage them but also, because they would take up a great deal of time and energy that could be better used doing something else. As well as these life-sustaining habits, our behavioural habits can be helpful too. They enable us to deal with the many tasks that confront us on a daily basis. Cleaning our teeth, taking a shower, getting dressed, driving the car and commuting to work are all examples of habits that enable us to be efficient and preserve energy.

Habits are formed because our brains seek patterns to automate. This tendency helps us, when the habits are 'good' and hinders us when our habits are 'bad'.

Every time we repeat a pattern of behaviour, a neural pathway is carved in the brain. The more often this happens, the more widely and deeply embedded in our brain that pathway becomes. In effect, it becomes 'the path of least resistance' through which our habits are formed and from which our choices disappear out of consciousness. This is why habits are so difficult to break. Sadly, the place in our brain that seeks repetitive patterns in order to form new habits doesn't discriminate. It just does its job, creating new habits wherever it can, making life easier and automating processes.

Happily, once conscious of this pathway, we can interrupt the automatic movement from stimulus to response and choose to do something different.

> *'Between stimulus and response there is a space. In that space is our power to choose our response. In our response lies our growth and our freedom.'*
>
> Stephen Covey, *The 7 Habits of Highly Effective People* (1994: 70)

inspired by:

> *'Everything can be taken from man but one thing: the last of the human freedoms – to choose one's attitude in any given set of circumstances, to choose one's own way.'*
>
> Viktor Frankyl, *Man's Search for Meaning* (2004: 75)

Stephen Covey goes on to say that using our self-awareness, our imagination, our moral compass and our will, we can chose our response to any given set of circumstances. Simple – in theory!

So, let's take a look at some of your social habits; the ones that show up as you being shy, and see if we can remove them from your repertoire by slowing down the speed of your automatic processing and choosing a different way.

What is it you find yourself doing repeatedly?

You probably have some of those 'Here I go again!' moments. These are the ones that you adopt habitually; the automatic behaviours that creep up on you and are 'out there' before you feel able to stop them. What are they? And what are the triggers that stimulate them? Try to be really specific. (A worked example is shown to help you on your way. Use the blank grid below the example and fill in your own.)

What is the automatic shy behaviour that you'd like to change?	 I'd like to stop myself from leaving social gatherings when I'm not speaking to anyone. At these times I feel foolish standing by myself and I lose my nerve. Once I start thinking that no one wants to talk to me and I that I have nothing interesting to say anyway, I just want to leave. So I do!
What is the trigger that creates this response?	 The trigger is when I think I'm 'supposed' to be professionally adequate or entertaining and I don't know many people.
In what situations do these triggers occur?	 This tends to happen when I'm at a party or a networking event where I carry a heavy expectation to be a good hostess or to represent myself professionally.

Now fill in your own:

What is the automatic shy behaviour that you'd like to change?	
What is the trigger that creates this response?	
In what situations do these triggers occur?	

It may be worth considering why the habits of shyness were laid down in the first place. Usually, these behaviours were adopted in response to the script of your upbringing and has more to do with the person doing the upbringing than you! As we have already discussed in Chapter 6, it is often conflicted and leaves you oscillating between two opposing social forces – 'Be charming!' versus 'Don't show off!' for instance. If this is the case, ask yourself who you are trying to please and whether they are still actively present in your life. If they're not, perhaps you could shed the injunctions and choose your own. If they are, perhaps you could plead 'choosing adult' and shed the injunctions anyway.

Activity 11.2

What are the consequences of your shyness?

We have talked about the 'rewards' you get for perpetuating your shyness. For instance: You may have got used to being rescued when you're feeling, or being, socially awkward. You may have got away with passing responsibility for a performance to someone who is prepared to do it for you. You may have been given special treatment to protect you from being socially exposed. Or you may avoid a mugging because you recede into the background! All of these examples are the 'benefits' of being shy. But there are other consequences, perhaps not so favourable: You may find yourself being passed over for promotion. You may lose out on fun and friendships. You may find yourself unable to reach the success you desire or live the life that you'd like to live. So, both positive and negative consequences flow from being shy. What are the consequences for you?

What are the consequences of your shyness in the context that contains your triggers, both positive and negative?	 I'm given special dispensation to leave professional gatherings early so that I don't have to socialize with people I don't know. The benefit of this is that I don't have to face situations in which I feel shy. The negative consequence is that I'm less likely to be involved in interesting things that may grow out of informal conversations.

And for you?

What are the consequences of your shyness in the context that contains your triggers, both positive and negative?	

Activity 11.3

What would you prefer to do?

Throughout this workbook, you've been invited into the worlds of other shy people. You've read of the experiences they've had and the things that they did to overcome their shyness in those specific instances. Looking back over all this material and incorporating all the thinking you've done, what tools and techniques have inspired you most and what would you like to do differently from now on?

What would you prefer to do in the context that you're thinking about?	I'd like to be in a conversational flow for at least half an hour longer than I usually am so that I can pick up on the less formal part of the proceedings. Perhaps go for a drink or dine with people I don't know very well.
What would be the advantage of doing this?	I may find that I make a connection with someone unexpectedly and that this leads to new ideas, new opportunities or new collaborations.

Now fill in your response below:

What would you prefer to do in the context that you're thinking about? This is your goal so make it SMART. (Specific, Measurable, Achievable, Realistic and Time-bound)	
What would be the advantage of doing this?	

Activity 11.4

What assumptions are you holding?

What assumptions are you holding that prevent you from doing what you'd prefer to do?

Using the Ladder of Inference to help you, see whether you can identify the assumptions or beliefs that hold you back from doing things differently. What assumption would you have to change to make it possible for you to move past this obstacle.

If you're having difficulty locating the assumption you hold that gets in the way, try asking yourself 'Why?' five times. For instance:

'Why do I leave social events?' – *Because I hate them.*

'Why do I hate them?' – *Because I always end up standing alone.*

'Why do I think that standing alone at an event is a problem?' – *Because it draws attention to me and highlights my inability to communicate*

'Why do I feel unable to communicate?' – *Because I don't know what to say.*

'Why don't I know what to say?' – *Because I think I'm boring.*

Then ask yourself:

'What assumption do I have to change to enable me to stay at social occasions?' – *I have to change the assumption that I'm boring and have nothing to say.*

What assumption or belief do you hold that gets in the way of you changing your behaviour?	*I assume that I'm boring and that no one will want to talk to me other than about work.*

What assumptions do you need to change to enable you to do what you'd prefer to do?	I need to assume that I can keep myself in communicative flow for longer than a passing exchange and that people will be interested in what I have to say.

Your turn…

What assumptions do you need to change to enable you to do what you'd prefer to do?	
What assumptions do you need to change to enable you to do what you'd prefer to do?	

Activity 11.5

How are you going to embed this new habit in your behaviour?

When you change a behaviour that people have got used to (indeed, they may be in a relationship with you *because* of your behaviour), they may try to encourage you back to the 'old you' that they knew and understood. For instance, someone who is only slightly less shy than you may rely upon you for companionship at an event. If you've overcome your shyness sufficiently to go off and network on your own, they'll have to deal with the consequences of that – and they may not like it! So, you may need to educate people that you really do want to overcome your shyness and that you'd appreciate their support.

So, before you try out your new behaviour, consider having a supporter who can encourage you, give you feedback and help you keep committed to the changes you want to make. This person could be someone who is at the same event as you or someone with whom you can debrief your experience afterwards – a coach, for instance or a trusted friend or colleague.

Then, think of the tools and techniques you're going to use to help you:

What is the tool or technique for overcoming shyness in this context that has inspired you as you've gone through this workbook?	I really liked the idea of being 'curious' and paying attention to someone else rather than feeling self-conscious and putting myself under pressure to 'perform'.
In which situations are you likely to apply it?	I could try this out at professional networking events; those where I have an opportunity to distinguish myself and build my reputation.

Your turn…

What is the tool or technique for overcoming shyness in this context that has inspired you as you've gone through this workbook?	
In which situations are you likely to apply it?	

What is your commitment to yourself?

Think about what you are going to do, precisely, so that you can measure your success. By having a clear idea about the tools and tactics you are going to use, you can review your experience and decide whether or not they will serve you in the long run or need adjusting so that they are sustainable for you. Below is an example of a plan.

What exactly are you going to do and when will you do it?	
	I have a networking event scheduled in three weeks' time. I will look at the delegate list and identify a couple of people that I'd like to speak to. I'll approach attendees to ask whether they know these people and whether they'd point them out or introduce me to them. I'll approach them, introduce myself, and state why I wanted to meet them. (Because I'm curious about...) I will be conscious of being curious during our conversation and ask lots of 'open' questions. If I'm invited to socialize afterwards, I will accept the invitation. (One day I may issue the invitation myself!)

What is your plan?

What exactly are you going to do and when will you do it?	

Activity 11.7

Closing the loop

When you have put your plan in place, check that you can answer the following questions:

▶ How did I know that I reached my goal?

Remember it was SMART – Specific, Measurable, Achievable, Realistic and Time-bound. For example:

▷ 'I'd like to be in a conversational flow for at least half an hour longer than I usually am so that I can pick up on the less formal part of the proceedings. Perhaps go for a drink or dine with people I don't know very well.'

▶ Which bit of it worked really well and can be used again?

▶ Which bit of it needs adjustment and testing out again?

▶ What feedback have I received that proves others have noticed my change in behaviour?

▶ On what date will I be using this approach next?

We already know that 'practice makes perfect'. So don't expect to be perfect without practising a few times. The learning ladder, shown below, is a way of conceiving the challenges of learning something new; learning to overcome your shyness, for instance.

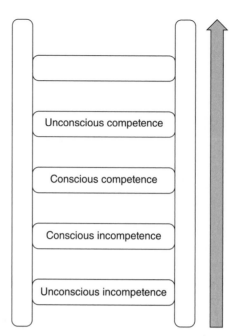

The learning ladder

As you step onto the first rung of the ladder, you are unaware of what you don't know. You are *unconsciously incompetent*.

However, because you've chosen this workbook on overcoming shyness, you are probably already on the second rung of the ladder where you are horribly *conscious* of your *incompetence!*

As you grapple with the material in this workbook and try out new things, you ascend to the next rung on the ladder. At this point, you are probably trying hard to 'get it right' and it may feel a bit unnatural but your learning has taken you forward and you are considered to be *consciously competent*.

Finally, as you become more familiar with the skills that you're developing, they begin to feel quite natural and they disappear out of consciousness. At this point, you are *unconsciously competent* and your behaviours are embedded in your natural repertoire.

So, don't expect to get up the ladder in one step. You will be experimenting with new behaviours and both reviewing and refining these constantly.

Where to next?

In this chapter, you've been encouraged to put some concrete into your commitment to overcome your shyness. You can use this approach over and over again with different behaviours in different circumstances so don't just sweep through the chapter once, return to it again and again until you know your assumptions and beliefs so well that you can select different responses to your triggers immediately.

The next chapter will comprise a toolkit that you can experiment with until you find one or two that work for you. Once you have overcome your own inertia and started making progress, you will find that the circle turns from vicious to virtuous and your learning will get easier and smoother until you find you have the confidence to take command of any social setting.

Don't forget to keep a note of your learning:

Keeping a note:	
What insights have you had as a result of reading this chapter?	

What are you going to
do differently as a result
of your insights?

12 Bringing it all together

Well, we have come to the end of this workbook. By now you will have had some insights about your particular form of shyness and found some ways to address it.

When you look back over the work you've done, you'll probably find that one or two points really hit home, while others were less inspiring to you.

There was no expectation that you should swallow this material whole, but that you would pick through the stories, the ideas, the tools and techniques to find ways that work for you. Even if you leave with just one or two powerful thoughts to actualize, you will be in more control of your social abilities than you were when you picked up this workbook and entered this field. And, hopefully, you will not stop here, but continue to think, experiment and learn more about yourself and how to preside over your own style of social engagement.

But before you go, it might be useful to dip back into the domain of your shyness and make sure that you have assimilated some of the main ways of addressing it. This distilled toolbox will ensure that you have the signposts that, progressively, show you the way to greater behavioural, emotional and rational autonomy. So, have a look at the four sections below and add any insights or activities that you feel are missing so that you have clarity around how you're going to think and what you're going to do differently.

→ Circumstantial/situational

Circumstantial and situational shyness has clear boundaries. It is quite possible to be extremely confident and outgoing in numerous situations but completely floored by giving a presentation, hosting an event or issuing an invitation (where a rejection would be mortifying). You will know, by now, that the higher level of uncertainty and exposure, the greater the potential for a shy reaction. So what do you do about this?

Seek as much certainty as possible by observing others doing the task that you dread and replicating what you think will work for you. By watching what they do, you'll be able to see if there is anything that you feel you could adopt, authentically.

Draw certainty from yourself in terms of what you say and try to bracket the context. This doesn't mean ignoring the nature of the occasion, but putting it to one side so that you are free to reveal what you know and talk about what you feel passionate about.

Enter the situation as often as you can. Avoidance is not the answer to circumstantial shyness. Practice makes perfect so look for opportunities to step into the field that you dread and develop some muscles so that you are less vulnerable to your shy reactions each successive time.

Do some scenario planning and include some contingency plans so that you always have somewhere to go should you need another resource or escape route. You could envisage the situation that you're about to enter, decide what's the best way of tackling it and practise your approach. Add a second tier to your plan for good measure.

Find someone you trust to run a role play or rehearsal with you. They could take your part (brief them well about your objective) and you could take the part of the person you're planning to 'target' (from a social perspective!) By putting yourself in someone else's shoes, by evoking them, you may find some clues about what approach would work best for them. Also, by watching someone taking your part, you may be inspired to try new things for yourself.

Do your research. If you are going to a networking event, try to get a list of attendees beforehand so that you can find some people that you'd like to talk to. If you're going to a conference, have a look at the programme and register for those sessions that interest you and to which you can contribute with a question or an insight. If it's a social occasion, think about who you will encounter and what kinds of conversation you can rely upon with them. Make sure that you have one or two interesting facts or comments about your points of mutual interest should you need them.

Set yourself tasks such as:

▶ Asking questions or making suggestions at a meeting

▶ Going into a room full of people you don't know and looking for connections whether they be people, places or interests

▶ Collecting business cards and a commitment for a follow-up meeting

▶ Accompany others in doing an activity that you are disinclined to do due to your shyness

▶ Initiating an event or organizing a party

- Find something you'd love to do and sign up for a class
- Put yourself online and start connecting with people who you have chosen to match your profile

Action plan
Date:
SMART goal:
The benefits to me of developing this new skill: (This will keep you motivated!)
My planned actions: (These are the specific actions that you aim to take.)

Key observations/insights/learning points:

Feedback: (This can be requested from anyone that you trust who was present and witnessed your action.)

Next steps:

→ Behavioural

As we have seen, behavioural shyness is described as the inability to respond skilfully or adapt to meet the demands of a situation. Social clumsiness, embarrassment, poor body language – including not being able to look people in the eye – and a quiet, uncertain or shaky voice are behavioural indicators of shyness. If this describes your type of shyness, have a look at the suggestions below to see whether there is anything of value in there for you.

Listen with curiosity to someone else rather than to your own, undermining, inner voice. Ask open questions and follow these up with further enquiry – although remember not to be inquisitional! By placing your attention, and interest, in someone else, you'll soon forget your own sense of inadequacy and your natural personality will have a chance to flow, unhindered, and engage others. This prevents the 'clunky', contrived behaviours (those that are consciously competent) that you might otherwise try to adopt to overcome your awkwardness.

Treat yourself as you would like to be treated and offer yourself the same respect that you would to others. This means being kind to yourself and forgiving any slight disappointments in your behaviour.

Develop some skills to help you. This may mean going to a presentation skills course, public speaking programme or singing lessons (so that you can manage the tone, pitch, pace and quality of your voice). Put yourself 'out there' as much as possible so that you have every opportunity to project yourself and your personality.

Seek feedback on how you come across. This might be with a coach or colleague with whom you have a good relationship. Sometimes it's hard to know how we are perceived yet, once we understand what we're doing to create the perceptions others' hold of us, we are able to 'renegotiate' these through adopting new behaviours or having different kinds of conversations, perhaps those where you 'name' what is going on for you and thereby dispel false beliefs.

Consider developing an assertive communication style. This is one where you respect your counterpart's position as much as your own.

It leads to mutuality and a win-win engagement – or adult-to-adult communication.

Try not to censor yourself too much. You have been gifted with a personality and a set of professional and personal interests. You have also been gifted with idiosyncrasies and eccentricities. The art is to be yourself, and to do it with conviction and without apology. So think about what you value about yourself, how you'd like to define yourself and factor these considerations into your behavioural strategies.

Learn how to build rapport. There are many tools that can help you achieve this, such as the following:

▶ Body language – observe others' body language and bring yours into alignment with theirs. (If they're sitting with their chin on the palm of their hand, gently mirror this.)

▶ Match their energy. This includes the speed with which they deliver their message. If they are animated and you are overly considered, it will feel like a mismatch to them.

▶ Listen out for the kind of language they use. Are they logical and precise or spontaneous and colourful? Do they use lots of descriptive terms or are they minimalist in their messaging? Do they evidence their responses with facts and figures or do they 'paint pictures' with their words? If you can reflect a similar conversational style back to them, you may find yourself making connections more easily.

▶ Give them lots of space to talk. Don't be afraid of the odd pause. Although it need only be a few seconds, it can create a space that they are inclined to fill.

▶ Try not to be too opinionated or try too hard to persuade them that you hold the correct view about something. Until you know someone well and the (tacit) rules of engagement have been established, it is dangerous to assume that they want the same kind of conversation as you do!

▶ Show empathy by demonstrating that you understand their position. For example, you might say something like: 'If I were you I'd feel…' Or 'When I was last in your situation, it occurred to me that…' Then ask: 'How do you feel about it?'

Initiate a conversation that you feel comfortable developing. Being proactive can make you feel more in control.

Action plan

Date:

SMART goal:

The benefits to me of developing this new skill: (This will keep you motivated!)

My planned actions: (These are the specific actions that you aim to take.)

Key observations/insights/learning points:

Feedback: (This can be requested from anyone that you trust who was present and witnessed your action.)

Next steps:

→ Emotional

Emotional shyness is triggered by the flight-or-fight response and results in physiological changes to the body. Panting, sweating, heavy breathing and digestive problems all fall under this category of shyness. Blushing, blanching and increased bowel activity are also part of this domain. As if this wasn't enough, very often the mind kicks in with negative self-talk: 'Here I go again, making a fool of myself!' And then a judgement: 'Everyone's going to think I'm nuts!'

Practise relaxation techniques until you find one that suits you best. *Visualization*, where you see yourself as if in a film conducting yourself as you would wish, or *relaxation*, where you learn to breathe and reduce the stress reaction in your body, are two useful approaches you may consider.

Try to avoid being a social perfectionist. If you look at others around you, you'll probably notice that they stammer, make clumsy gestures, blush and apologize for themselves – and they just carry on regardless. Try to move on if you make what you believe to be a social faux pas and just file it for future reference.

Our colour naturally rises when we laugh or smile. When you are embarrassed and aware that your face is reddening, try to smile, with conviction, to disguise your colour and make you feel less self-conscious. (Be careful not to overuse this tactic!)

If you are in a meeting or at a social gathering, try to make an early intervention so that you are familiar with the sound of your voice in that setting. The longer you wait to speak, the higher is the emotional barrier that you have to overcome. Hearing your voice break the silence early makes it possible to return to say more.

Be comfortable in your clothes. When you put on a costume, make sure that it does not feel alien to you and that you can function naturally. It is best to avoid any potential wardrobe malfunction.

Learn how to flood yourself with feelings of self-esteem and positivity when you need to. Having anchored a time when you were feeling in command of your social behaviours, you can recall this at will to change your state from shy to confident. (This technique was described in Chapter 8.)

Develop your self-awareness to the point where you recognize when you are slipping into your fear.

Notice what happens when your flight-or-fight response is triggered and your physiology takes over.

Tune into yourself acutely so that you can 'read' your response and choose another route.

Channel your nervous energy into something more creative; a displacement activity such as:

- ▶ Offering to fetch someone another drink
- ▶ Introducing your counterpart to someone they haven't yet met
- ▶ Excusing yourself for a moment while you 'refresh' yourself
- ▶ Breathing deeply to dispel the tensions you are experiencing in your body

Stand your ground. Use your body to create a stable structure that would be hard to shift. That means standing with your feet planted firmly, shoulder distance apart, and arms by your side.

Surround yourself with a circle of good friends who are prepared to act as sounding boards to relieve you of your anxieties and remind you of your social tactics.

Call to mind something of greater importance that sits beyond what you're currently doing. Doing this will help you reduce the 'charge' that the situation engenders and help you gain a meaningful perspective. It will also create a bridge that will carry your focus away from your punishing self-talk.

Action plan
Date:
SMART goal:
The benefits to me of developing this new skill: (This will keep you motivated!)

My planned actions: (These are the specific actions that you aim to take.)

Key observations/insights/learning points:

Feedback: (This can be requested from anyone that you trust who was present and witnessed your action.)

Next steps:

→ Rational

As a reminder, rational (or irrational) shyness is thought-based. In this form of shyness, the habitual patterns of thought that dominate the mind are automatically played. (Which perhaps suggests that they are 'thought-less'!) They can be based upon past experiences that have become 'facts of life' or they can speculate a future that constructs a set of fears. Whatever, these cognitions are fixed and repetitive. Sometimes they are helpful, such as determining when to take flight. Other times, they steal our choice and autonomy by undermining our agency. If these thought patterns are knocking about in your head and preventing you from appraising each situation in the present, here are some suggestions:

Be present. You will be left with few resources if you are distracted by the past (which is no longer happening) or the future (which hasn't happened yet). Try to discipline your mind to attend to what's happening now. If you hear those old messages creeping in, just pay them no attention and bring your focus back to something in front of you. This will take practice but you can control your mind. It doesn't have to control you!

Use visualization to program your subconscious to bring to fruition what you desire. Hold an image of yourself engaging confidently with people and managing the ebb and flow of a social situation with grace and ease.

Don't procrastinate or hesitate. Step forward and take a risk. People who spend most of their time in their heads tend to think things through from every angle before taking the plunge. Once you've cast your inner eye over the most significant aspects of the situation you're in, forget the analysis and just be curious about what other people think. Once you've asked the first open question, the process will have started and all you have to do is listen carefully and remain attentive.

Use mindful techniques to manage the importance you place upon people and events. Making the image of people and things smaller in your mind will reduce the power they have over you. Creating distance between you and the things that you fear will give you a greater sense of command.

Give people the benefit of the doubt. Shy people who construct conversations in their heads tend to err on the side of negativity and imagine others judging them harshly. It is just possible that, at the same time that you think they are judging you, they are actually judging themselves. There are far more shy people 'out there' than we credit. Figures of around 50 per cent have been bandied about by various researchers so the chances are, they haven't got the head space to do you as much disservice as you do yourself!

Build your self-esteem. Write down all the things that you value and appreciate about yourself. The more you can build this essential psychic foundation, the more you will be able to withstand the vicissitudes of life.

Root out the negative self-talk. There are probably several layers of this that go on at the same time and block out more positive feedback loops. Remind yourself:

- ▶ You are not the only person that people will be watching.
- ▶ They do not have access to your inner thoughts and fears.
- ▶ You are bound to be harder on yourself than anyone else can be.
- ▶ You are probably doing more things 'right' than 'wrong'.
- ▶ You can show your full personality without adverse effects.
- ▶ People are much more forgiving than you think.

Sometimes, when you blush, it doesn't show!

Action plan
Date:
SMART goal:
The benefits to me of developing this new skill: (This will keep you motivated!)

My planned actions: (These are the specific actions that you aim to take.)

Key observations/insights/learning points:

Feedback: (This can be requested from anyone that you trust who was present and witnessed your action.)

Next steps:

Well, that's it. You have now come full circle and have explored the territory that is your shyness.

The most important thing is to make your choices so that you can live a rich and fulfilled life and enjoy yourself while you're doing it. Anything that gets in the way is sapping your energy so make a decision to overcome your shyness and discipline yourself to stick with it until you reap the rewards.

Good luck!

References

Covey, S. R. *The 7 Habits of Highly Effective People – Powerful lessons in personal change* (Simon & Schuster, 1994)

Csíkszentmihályi, M. *Flow: The psychology of optimal experience* (Harper Perennial Modern Classics, 2008)

Frankl, V. E. *Man's Search for Meaning* (Ebury Publishing, 2004)

Gladwell, M. *Outliers: The Story of Success* (Back Bay Books, 2011)

Lakoff, G.; Johnson, M. *Metaphors We Live By* (University Of Chicago Press; 2nd edition, 2003)

Peters, Dr S. *The Chimp Paradox: The mind management programme to help you achieve success, confidence and happiness* (Vermilion, 2012)

Rodenburg, P. *The Second Circle: How to use positive energy for success in every situation* (W. W. Norton & Company, 2008)

Senge, P. M.; Scharmer, O. C; Jaworski, J.; Flowers, B. S. *Presence: Human Purpose and the Field of the Future* Paperback (Crown Business, 2008)

van der Molen, H. T. Chapter 9: A definition of shyness and its implications for clinical practice in: Crozier, W. R. *Shyness and Embarrassment: Perspectives from Social Psychology* (Cambridge University Press, 2011)

Index